10

Dear Mom and Dad
parents and the preschooler

Dear Mom and Dad
parents and the preschooler

Barbara J. Taylor

Brigham Young University Press

Taylor, Barbara J.
  Dear mom and dad

  Bibliography: p.
  1. Child development. 2. Parent and child.
3. Education, Preschool—1965– I. Title.
LB1115.T24   372.21   78-5121

ISBN 0-8425-1231-4

Brigham Young University Press, Provo, Utah 84602
© 1978 by Brigham Young University Press. All rights reserved
Printed in the United States of America
5Mp 5/78 30951

Table of Contents

NOTE: For purposes of clarity and ease of language, the pronoun he has been used to refer to the individual child in this book. This in no way implies that the child being discussed is a boy; the principles in this book apply equally to boys and girls, and it is equally important that parents work with both their sons and their daughters. It is unnecessary to try and tackle simultaneously all of the activities and concepts expressed here. Don't become overwhelmed by all of the suggestions contained in this book—work with your child at his pace of development, and participate with him in the activities one at a time. Don't worry if some of the activities don't seem to be applicable to or practical for your child—the activities listed here are universal in nature, but may have to be tailored slightly to fit individual needs. Although an activity may be mentioned in only one section, most activities overlap and can be applied to other principles in other sections.

One

Physical (Motor) Development

A Note from Your Preschooler

Dear Mom and Dad,

Every day I will get bigger and better. Don't worry about what I can't do today. I will be able to do things better and faster as my body grows and as it gets used to doing different things.

I can do things with my big muscles now; later I will be able to do things with my little muscles. Sometimes my body shouts at me and tells me to run and jump over my toys, climb up on the furniture, or wiggle all over. Then it's harder than you think for me to sit still and draw, listen to stories, or cut out pictures. You can help me feel good about my body and the way I use it; then I'll feel better about my thoughts, too. And I'll have more fun with my friends. I won't need to show off.

I'm not being bad when I'm being curious. I want you to like me, but I need to find out things, too. My world is so exciting.

If I feel good about my body, I like the rest of me, too. When I do things well, I feel good. But having to keep up with others all the time makes me sad; losing isn't any fun, and when you compare me with others it makes me mad. Please love me, because I'm special.

Sometimes I won't do very well. You may know that I can act better, but sometimes I am not quite sure of myself. The world is a big place full of new and scary things. Be patient with me and help me.

I will try to be like you. If you're happy about how my body is growing, I will be, too. More than anybody else, you can help me to grow right and have fun.

Thanks for spending time with me. It makes a big difference.
     Love,
     Your Preschooler

1

Introduction

Think back to the first two questions everyone asked you when your child was born: "Is it a boy or a girl?" "How much did it weigh?" Both questions concern physical characteristics, and physical development really should be considered first—it provides the base for your child's successful intellectual, emotional, social, and moral growth.

Physical growth is directional: a child develops from head to toes and from the axis (center) of the body outward. A child raises his head before he sits, and a child stands before he walks. Whole arm movements are used to corral objects before the thumb and fingers are combined to pick them up. This characteristic of growth relates to two types of motor development: large (or gross) muscle, which concerns movement and balance of the whole body; and small (or fine) muscle, which concerns hand movements, eye-hand coordination, and so on.

When a child is learning to develop large- and small-muscle coordination, his body movements may be smooth or jerky, confident or hesitant. Because motor skills are used throughout his life, the child must feel good about his body and its abilities.

Motor abilities have both cause and effect relationships with other aspects of development such as vision, speech, reading readiness, and reading achievement. A concerned adult can provide a preschooler with stimulation of the five senses and can train him in left-right discrimination by using games and activities. A close relationship exists between motor-skill development, a sense of total body image, and success in later complex learning. From the autonomous (or self-directing) behavior of a two-and-a-half-year-old, one can successfully predict his nonverbal or demonstrated intelligence and thinking style at age six (Pederson and Wender 1968). A two-and-a-half-year-old who shows independence and persistence in play will become a six-year-old who demonstrates problem-solving abilities. The younger children who seek physical contact and attention tend to seek these same things at age six (Smart and Smart 1973).

General Guidelines for Physical Development

Because physical growth and maturation are prerequisites for success in other areas, you should be aware of what normal growth is and how you can properly care for your preschooler's developing body; you should know what you can expect of your child's physical growth, skeletal system, internal organs, sleep patterns, and societal adjustment.

You can easily observe your child's physical growth from the earliest weeks. An infant gains four to seven ounces per week, and by age one has generally tripled his birth weight. Although the rate of weight gain decreases from ages one to three, it accelerates gradually again from three to five. Girls usually reach one-half of their adult height before the age of two; boys reach one-half of their adult height by age two. It takes four years to double the birth height, and about sixteen years to reach the final height (Watson and Lowrey 1967; Smart and Smart 1973).

The preschool child's body is constantly changing in composition. He has more cartilage in his skeletal system and fewer mineral deposits in the bones than an adult does. His joints are very flexible, but his ligaments and muscles are not firmly attached. For these reasons his skeletal system can be easily damaged from pressure, pulling, infection, malnutrition, fatigue, and injury. Swinging or lifting the infant or preschool child by the hands, even though he begs for and enjoys it, can be harmful.

The child's internal organs need care, too. Proper nutrition and feeding habits are vital; food and nutrition are discussed later in this chapter.

As further protection for the child's developing organs, serious illness should be prevented. The preschooler's developing body can be severely damaged by diseases such as diphtheria, pertussis (whooping cough), tetanus, polio, red measles, mumps, and rubella (three-day measles). Immunizations are available to prevent all of these diseases, but unfortunately many young parents who don't remember the devastating effects of polio and other epidemics fail to protect their children. Pediatricians and local immunization clinics provide protection against these diseases at low cost.

The preschooler may also be especially susceptible to colds and sore throats, as well as have difficulty in breathing, because the tonsils and adenoids are at their maximum size and the child's air passages are small.

Regular sleep and rest are necessary for proper growth, but sleep patterns may be harder to establish than other patterns such as feeding. When the child is highly stimulated, when time and procedure for sleep are irregular, and when you are inconsistent, the child will more likely reject your requests for him to go to sleep. It is easier for the child to retire when he is not excited, when there is a regular routine, and when you are firm but affectionate. Compare these situations:

Bedtime arrives. You tell your preschooler to get ready for bed; arguments follow. "I want to play longer," "I haven't heard my new book," or "My favorite show is starting" are usual pleas. You give in to first one thing and then another—reminding the child to get ready for bed between each change of event. Your child wonders if even *you* know what you expect. Every night it's the same battle.

The second situation: bedtime arrives. You tell your preschooler to finish playing and put the toys away. You suggest a story *or* a game (a regular ritual) when the child is in his pajamas. The child makes a choice. You remind him to get a drink, go to the bathroom, or get a sleeping toy before he retires. The bedtime routine is enjoyable and consistent. You both know what is expected.

A child may be disturbed by dreams because he does not have the ability to distinguish them from reality; if you provide warm reassurance in his own room it will encourage sleep. Taking the child into your bed or intensifying the incident may increase his desire for reassurance. If your preschooler has a frightening dream and awakens in the night, go to him and listen to his concerns. It is useless and unrealistic to try to convince the child that the dream didn't happen; it is very real to him. Talk calmly and understandingly. If necessary, turn on the lights and look around. Try to see the situation from the child's point of view. After reassuring the child, leave a light on in the hall or lay down beside him until he falls asleep. When you take the child to bed with you, you are implying that the dream might have been true, and you are failing to help the child resolve the problem.

Society will expect a young child to be able to perform certain tasks (sitting alone, walking, talking, interacting, and so on) at certain ages. If he doesn't meet the "normal" timetable, it may be because of developmental retardation or immaturity, lack of an opportunity to practice or learn, or lack of motivation. At any rate, failure to meet society's expectations may lead to unhappiness and feelings of inferiority, social disapproval or rejection, and further delay in new developmental skills. The more children fall behind expectations, the more discouraged they become. The more they perform at expected levels, the happier and more confident they feel. Be patient with your child. If you have reason to suspect exceptionally slow or inappropriate behavior, check with professional sources such as your pediatrician, state or local agencies, universities, or private clinics.

How to Help Your Preschooler's Physical Development

Parents and teachers should remember certain general rules about growth and maturation: (1) a preschooler's physical development is a correlated, predictable sequence with fast and slow periods and wide variation among individuals; (2) the child should be able to perform certain tasks at certain times during his development according to the expectations of society; (3) development comes through readiness based on maturation and learning; and (4) because development follows a predictable pattern, a child can successfully be prepared now to learn better and to adjust more easily in the future.

Parents should be careful before adopting motor or "movement education" programs that have appeared in recent years (such as those developed by Cratty, Delacato, Getman, Kephart, and Laban, for example). Some of these programs have come under attack by researchers, educators, and medical doctors who charge that the programs are based on false principles, make unproven claims, and are even harmful to young children (Cratty 1970; Hendrick 1975). If you're thinking of trying out a motor education program on your child, find out about it first: read about it, talk about it with knowledgeable professionals, and then make your decision with *your* child in mind. Don't get taken in by the fads. Don't involve your child in a program because you want him to do something sooner or better than the child next door. *Do* become informed on normal development patterns. *Do* spend time with your child so he can grow happily in a healthy atmosphere at his own rate.

After learning these basic facts about your preschooler's physical-motor development, you are probably already wondering what you can do to help. Following are discussions and lists of activities to help your child achieve mastery of his body concerning large-muscle (gross) motor development, small-muscle (fine) motor development, left-right (bilateral) motor development, and proper utilization of food and nutrition.

Large-muscle (Gross Motor) Development

Attitudes and Abilities

You have undoubtedly noticed that one of the most important aspects of development during the preschool years is mobility and action. You may often wonder where the child gets so much energy.

Learning to move around on his own (or developing a "sense of autonomy," as Erikson calls it) is very important to the young child. He is just as anxious for his motor development to occur as you are. Such development contributes to enjoyment, socialization, self-concept, good health, independence, and other positive characteristics. If a child can successfully develop motor skills, he will also develop self-trust and will avoid shame and doubt about his new abilities. For a child, being able to do things on his own—no matter how long they take or how well they're done—feels so good. "I dressed myself this morning," a pleased preschooler announces proudly, appearing in mismatched socks, pants that are on backwards, and a color combination representative of a spring rainbow. "I emptied the garbage just for you," announces another, as you note egg shells, cans, fruit peelings, and crumpled paper trailing in a distinct path from the kitchen to the outside garbage can.

Children often lack the experience or the necessary skills to perform tasks as well as they want to, so an encouraging word or demonstration from you can be reassuring. Don't tell your child he can't do something; instead, offer positive suggestions, provide opportunities, and show your appreciation for your child's successful experiences. With such encouragement your child will continue to try—and to learn. Say, "It really is hard for your fingers to work the scissors and cut the paper, but I'm glad you tried. Each time it gets easier," or, "There were so many toys scattered around your room that it takes a long time to stack them on the shelf. You did such a good job," or, "It's hard for one person to wipe all that water up off the floor. I'll get a sponge and help, too." Statements like these show respect, encouragement, and appreciation.

In developing the motor skills your child needs to feel competent, he begins with the large muscles. The last time you noticed preschool children at play, they were probably using the large muscles—walking, running, jumping, skipping, throwing, swinging, and so on.

Developing good stationary balance (like balancing on one foot) reflects the efficiency, integration, and control of the muscular system, eyes, and inner ear (Cratty 1970). Your child must also continually adjust and reorganize his posture as he grows.

If muscles develop normally, your child's respect for self and others

increases and he learns faster. Also, many experts have found a strong relationship between motor and mental abilities (Lillie 1975). Large-muscle coordination, one of the first skills acquired, provides the basis for future, more complex learning.

You should provide many activities to increase your child's large-muscle development. If you don't want your child jumping on your furniture, find an old mattress or tire. For example, show the preschooler how to safely jump by helping him jump off a low step or over a low board where there is plenty of space. A child will eventually jump anyway, so give him some appropriate guidelines. The parent who says, "I just won't let you jump" is telling the child that the experience is fearful, that his body is inferior, and that the adult is in control.

Other inexpensive activities can also be easily provided and are listed at the end of this section under "Activities for Large-Muscle Development (Gross Motor Skills)."

Normal Development Patterns

When your child is eighteen months old, perfecting his walking skills is most important to him. Generally by age two, he can walk sideways and backwards, and at three he can walk on tiptoe. At four most children can walk on a narrow elevated plank and retain balance most of the time. At four a child can also run and play games (such as riding a stick horse) without too many falls. It is still rather difficult for a four-year-old to jump over obstacles (such as boards and boxes), but with a little more time and practice he will be able to hurdle such objects—and will be able to jump rope by age six. Skipping and hopping, however, are complex skills so much more difficult that the child won't be able to accomplish them successfully before the age of six or seven. He can ascend and descend stairs in the adult manner (each foot alternately) by the age of four if adequate experience has been provided him. Swimming is a highly coordinated skill that few children can do well before the age of four. Given an opportunity, most preschoolers can pedal a tricycle satisfactorily by the age of four, and many children can ride a bicycle by the time they are six, according to studies by Hurlock. The preschool child enjoys being pushed in a swing mainly because he gets lots of attention without having to work hard; actually, a swing is not a good gross-motor skill developer until the child grows older, has better body coordination, and can move his legs to pump the swing.

While the child grows only half as much between three and five years of age as he did between the ages of one and three, following the fifth birthday his body movements become more integrated and his bilateral action improves. The child may move his arms when he is jumping or throwing, thus using the proper weight shift. Even so, ball handling will be immature and inconsistent because throwing and catching abilities are relatively undeveloped; a child may throw a ball underhand, side-arm, or occasionally overhand, and can catch a *large* ball. The five-year-old can jump about one foot in the air, can broad-jump about three feet, and can balance in place (standing on one or both feet) and in motion (walking on a board or jumping from one place to another). He can run in a well-coordinated manner. He needs lots of experiences to perfect these movement abilities.

Common Variations in Development Patterns

Children of the same chronological age are widely different in large-motor skills, interests, and abilities. One child may be able to climb with good coordination and speed while another may be hesitant to step on even a low board. One child may skip and do acrobatics while another may run cautiously or rely on adult help.

Remember that motor development (or skill learning) cannot occur until the child is maturationally ready. Parts of the child's body (motor areas of the brain, the nervous system, the muscles, and others) must be developed before specific skills are possible.

In tests of large-muscle coordination, boys are likely to do better than girls at all ages, but girls show early superiority in manual dexterity (such as drawing, cutting, and stringing). In comparing boys and girls between the ages of two and six, boys excel in ladder and step climbing, in jumping, and in catching, throwing, and bouncing balls. Girls do better in hopping, skipping, and galloping (see Smart and Smart 1973). Keep in mind that the variations among children aged two to six are wide and that these generalities may not necessarily apply to your child. The *pattern* of motor development is predictable—the *skills* your child will have at a certain age are not predictable.

Even though there are cultural and developmental expectations, some children reach these standards earlier or later than others. Children who deviate widely from the norm could do so from lack of experience, interest, motivation, or maturation. If parents seriously question a child's development, they should seek advice from public or private agencies.

Activities for Large-Muscle Development (Gross Motor Skills)

You can help your child's large-muscle development by providing certain activities. He really doesn't need elaborate or expensive equipment; he does need basic pieces, lots of space, and plenty of time, elements that are important for vigorous, energetic, physical play. Following is a list of suggested activities that would be easy for you and fun for your child.

Activities to Do Outside

Run
  As individuals or while playing games

Crawl
  Around the yard to find objects hidden by an adult.
  Through objects (boxes, obstacle course); under objects (table, rope); around objects (tree, box); and over objects (pillow, box).
  Behind a person or along a course made by chalk or a string.

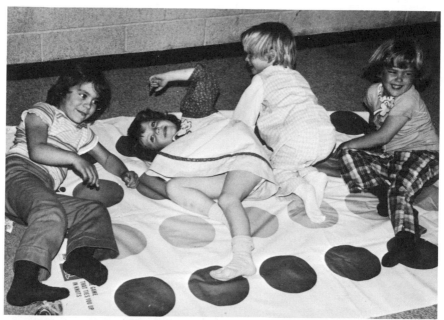

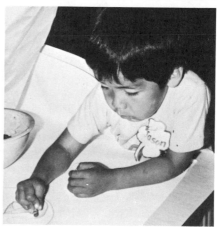

Over a replica of a community drawn by an adult on a large sheet of
paper or cloth (an old sheet, canvas, or cardboard is good), arranging objects (cars, houses, trees, or people) on the replica
while crawling.

Jump

By crouching down, then jumping up with arms extended (like a
jack-in-the-box or popcorn in a hot pan).

Over small things (can, string, line), perhaps pretending to be Jack-
Be-Nimble.

Up to touch or reach something (leaf, toy, balloon).

From a standing position (perhaps pretending to be a Mexican jumping bean), from place to place, shape to shape, or color to color.

By imitating jumping animals (frog, kangaroo, rabbit).

On trampolines, tires, old mattresses.

Over low objects while running, pretending to jump "across the riv-
er."

Walk or step

In to and out of tires, hoops, or circles.

On low boards or on a line, string, or rope.

On raised boards.

On wide surfaces (newspaper), gradually progressing to narrow surfaces (string).

Through a maze, following a course by holding onto a guide (rope or
string).

On top of footsteps cut out of paper (could lead to an area out of the
child's sight).

Forward and backward alternately while playing games such as
"Mother, May I?," "Follow the Leader," "Do as I'm Doing."

While pretending to be on various structures (fence, bridge, rope) or
various materials (egg shells, gum, hot rocks, soft sand).

While following instructions ("Walk around in a circle, . . . backwards,
. . . fast").

While imitating walking patterns of animals (duck, dog).

To various tempos of music.

Around the neighborhood or community.

Climb

Along an obstacle course.

Up a ladder.

Up a rope with large knots tied about every twelve inches. Child
grabs one knot, pulls himself up to sit on it, and then pulls himself
up to the next one.

Up steps.

Over sawhorses, large blocks, ropes, tires, fences, or barrels.

While hiking.

Up a hill, up a tree, or over a small shed.

Kick

While aiming at a ball or target.
At balloons or pillows.
By swinging foot at a suspended object.
By swinging leg to music.

Hop

Only on certain colors or shapes (everything green, everything square, and so on).
As hopping animals do.
On toes only rather than on the whole foot.
In an "Indian war dance"—hop twice on each foot before changing to the other.
As many times as possible on each foot.

Skip

To music. (This bilateral activity will be difficult for most preschool children, but let them practice as you give verbal instructions.)
To various rhythms.
Alone or while holding another's hand.

Balance

On one foot until a bell rings or the music stops.
On one foot in a large square. (As the child becomes more proficient, the squares should be made smaller and smaller.)
By squatting or stooping (like a squirrel with a nut or like toys in box).
While walking on narrow board or line.
By standing with feet close together and arms extended.

Use arms

By stretching and reaching for objects (limb, sky).
By dressing up for dramatic play.
By swinging from a bar.
By throwing bean bags, balloons, balls, airplanes, or an old sock filled with foam or fabric. (Try to think of games such as knocking blocks down from a distance, throwing objects through an opening, playing catch, throwing objects over a barrier, playing with a magnetic game, or using suction darts.)
By rolling objects (cars, tires, balls).
By playing "catch" with large objects.
By painting. (Use a small-sized roller and a shallow pan filled with poster paint or water. Or use a large paint brush and a can. Let the child paint a large cardboard box or use the water to "paint" surfaces that are not harmed by moisture.)
By manipulating a balloon or paper streamer through the air.
By tossing a frisbee.
By nailing bottle caps onto a board or making a shaker out of them.
By building with large blocks, cans, or boxes.
By bouncing balls.

By pushing wheel toys (wagons, wheelbarrows).
By lifting and hauling objects.
By playing in sand and dirt.
By hitting a punching bag.

Practice coordinated movements
On an obstacle course.
By stepping in to and out of tires, hoops, and circles.
By marching.
By doing situps.
By manipulating wheel toys (cars, wheelbarrows, riding toys).
By imitating animal movements.
By jumping.
By galloping with and without a stick horse.
By playing "Freeze." (The child moves freely until someone says the word "Freeze," and then the child holds that position until he is told to move again.)
By making angels. (The child lies on his back in snow, sand, grass, or on the carpet with his arms and legs extended, and he moves his arms and legs outward to make a design like an angel.)
By playing simplified baseball. (The pitcher tosses a ball or object; the batter catches it, throws it, and then runs to base.)
By playing games with adults. (The adult says, "Watch what I can do," and then demonstrates. The child imitates, and then they switch roles.)
By attaching small bells to pieces of elastic or ribbon and tying them to the child's wrists or ankles. (Encourage the child to make various rhythms by moving his hands and legs.)
By riding a tricycle or pedal car.
By doing acrobatic tricks (keeling over, rolling, and so on).
By playing records or tapes.
By preparing soil and planting seeds.
By watering house plants.

Activities to Do Together

Play games

"Follow the Leader," "Do as I Am Doing," "Mother, May I?"

Exercise

Walk, run, jump, hop, and so on.

Go for a walk or hike.

(Also see many of the ideas listed under "Activities To Do Outside," "Activities That Require Props," and "Activities To Do Inside.")

Activities That Require Props

Follow obstacle courses: boxes, boards, string, rope, and ladders.

Jump: trampoline, tires, hoops, and boxes.

Throw: balls, bean bags, pillows, and suction darts.

Dig: sand, dirt, flour, sawdust, and good tools.

Paint: water or paint, brushes, and containers.

Pretend or have dramatic play: dress-ups, jewelry, hats, and shoes; cleaning equipment, brooms, and mops; dolls; and trucks.

Cook: food, pans, utensils, rolling pins, and heat.

Hit and pound: clay, punching bag, wood and tools (soft wood, workable tools, and medium-sized nails), and knock-out bench.

Play records and tapes.

Activities to Do Inside

Crawl: see "Activities To Do Outside," and apply them to indoor areas.

Jump: see "Activities To Do Outside," and apply them to indoor areas.

Exercise: do situps, rolls, toe and knee touching, and so on.

Throw: bean bags, pillows, and magnetic objects.

Walk: on crepe paper, string, yarn, low boards, and so on.

Move arms: reaching, swinging.

Dramatize: provide props, ideas, space, and time.

Cook: prepare and serve food, prepare tables and areas for snacks or meals, turn an ice cream freezer, use utensils, beat, squeeze, roll, grind, sift, and stir.

Clean: scrape, wash, and dry dishes; mop and sweep the floor; dust; polish; spray and water.

Build: use large blocks, cans, boxes, and props (chairs, sheets, and so on).

Activities That Are Simple, Inexpensive, Versatile, and Fun

Use bean bags: walk while balancing one or more bags (on head, foot, shoulder, or back of extended hand; walk holding bean bag between knees; crawl while balancing bean bag on back, shoulder, or head).

Run modified relay races.

Toss bean bag through openings (clown face, large cans, tire, or hoop).

Play a game. Cut the bottoms out of two plastic containers (three-quart or gallon) that have side handles. Scoop and throw a bean bag to a

partner, who catches it in a container and scoops it back.

Toss the bean bag into the air and catch it, or toss and exchange the bag simultaneously with a partner, or toss and chase the bag.

Toss the bag underhand and then overhand.

Use a rope:

Walk on it.

Use the rope as a guide (to lead the child from one place or activity to another).

Jump over the rope at different heights.

Make designs with the rope (straight line, circle, or letter).

Use the rope as a jumping rope as the child's abilities increase.

Tie simple knots.

Pull objects such as a wagon or box with the rope.

Wrap the rope around objects (pole, box).

Use a hoop (hula and other sizes):

Jump over the hoop.

Crawl through the hoop.

Use the hoop in an obstacle course.

Use the hoop as a child's "own space," in which tricks and other activities are performed.

Ask the child to sit in the hoop and put various parts of his body outside of it as you call the names of the parts (toe, head, arm).

Have the child jump from one hoop into another.

Have the child toss a bean bag or pillow into a hoop.

Put hoops so they overlap each other. Ask the child to step from one hoop into the next (vary the distance from very close to far apart).

Have the child try swinging his hoop around the various parts of his body (waist, neck, arm, leg).

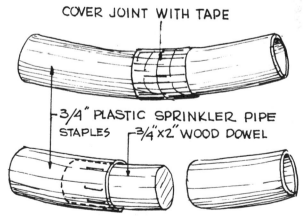

COVER JOINT WITH TAPE

3/4" PLASTIC SPRINKLER PIPE

STAPLES ⌐3/4"x2" WOOD DOWEL

PUSH PIPES TOGETHER OVER DOWEL, STAPLE THROUGH PIPE INTO WOOD. COVER WITH TAPE

HULA HOOP JOINT DETAIL

Small-Muscle (Fine Motor) Development

Attitudes and Abilities

It is a long, slow process for the child to learn how to manipulate the small muscles in his hands and arms with any precision. The preschooler is just beginning to move his fingers and wrists quickly and flexibly; his hands and arms are just beginning to hold things more steadily. The child is often frustrated because his hands and fingers won't do what he wants them to: his fingers are unsteady as he tries to thread objects; scissors don't cut; puzzle pieces need to be turned; and his fingers and hands aren't very strong yet.

Remind yourself that growth proceeds from near to far—from the center axis of the body toward the extremities. The infant used to corral things with his hands and arms; the preschooler can now oppose his thumb and fingers to pick up objects more easily.

The child's small muscles are still so immature that it's hard for him to sit still during a difficult or uninteresting activity, such as when he is coloring, cutting, or arranging objects. But fine motor skills and eye-hand coordination improve with practice. For a fun and simple eye-hand experience when the child wants to start pouring, let him pour beans (or some other large and easily cleaned up substance) from one container into a second wide-mouthed container (large plastic measuring cups with handles are good). As the child masters this task, gradually reduce the size of the substance (from wheat or rice to salt to water, for example), and then gradually reduce the size of the pitcher and the container.

Your preschooler wants to work with materials that are enjoyable, interesting, and easy to manipulate (such as fingerpaints, clay, or unstructured toys). Although he will need your help in terminating an activity *before* he becomes discouraged (he will become tense, push things away or onto the floor, become careless, and so on), good emotional release can result from carefully planned small-muscle activities such as pasting, tearing or crumbling paper, or cutting through soft things like bananas or bread with a knife.

Normal Development Patterns

Like gross motor development, fine motor development follows a general pattern that varies in specifics with each individual child. When a child is about five months old, he can grasp and hold on to an object but he can't voluntarily release it; he brushes it against the body or against another object until it is knocked out of his hand. An eight-month-old can oppose thumb and fingers in picking up objects, but his attempts are awkward. Gradually muscles develop until there is good control at times over certain activities. The child can pick up and release small objects like cereal, pegs, and toys. The muscles of the arms, shoulders, and wrists should be near adult performance by twelve years. Finger muscles develop much more slowly, so that a child can't write rapidly or play a musical instrument effectively until twelve or older.

DEVELOPMENTAL MILESTONES IN DRAWING AND WRITING SKILLS		
At the completion of:	Drawing Skills	Writing Skills
Preschool	Holds and manipulates writing utensil (fat crayons and pencils for small fingers).	
3-year-old	Can execute a complete circle.	
4-year-old	Can execute a square.	Prints haphazardly all over page, his letters are in all directions.
5-year-old		Can begin to print his own name.
6-year-old		Progresses rapidly and should be able to print the alphabet, his first and last name, and numbers one through ten.
6½- or 7-year-old	Can execute a triangle and a cross.	

Reference: Cratty, 1970

You can help your child develop fine motor skills and a positive attitude toward them. Encourage self-feeding by providing lots of finger foods (apple slices, raw vegetables, toast strips, and so on). Make sure clothing is easy to manipulate—provide zippers or large buttons instead of snaps, elastic instead of small buttons or ties, front rather than back openings—and encourage self-dressing. The five-year-old should be able to completely dress himself except for tying shoes, which should generally be mastered by the age of six. Dressing oneself takes good eye-hand coordination, as does grooming. To help your child develop skills and reliance in self-dressing, combine the above suggestions with a procedure for helping the child decide on which clothes he wants to wear: the night before, help the child set out his clothes for morning. It will then be easy for the child to dress himself in the morning.

Before entering kindergarten (generally age five), the child should be able to brush or comb his hair with little help from you. The five-year-old will want to bathe himself and brush his own teeth, but knows that sometimes you need to help him with "tough" jobs like lacing shoes, cleaning fingernails, parting hair, tying bows, and buttoning small buttons.

Even though the preschooler will want to use crayons or writing utensils and will make rough attempts to write, his body is not biologically ready for handwriting until the age of six. Before then, the nerves and muscles of the fingers, hands, wrists, and arms are so undeveloped that the fine movements required in writing are difficult (Hurlock 1972). For a good preparatory experience with writing utensils, you can give the child large crayons and large sheets of plain paper so he can explore and experiment.

As the preschooler develops the necessary skills to hold and manipulate writing utensils (fat crayons and pencils are easier for small fingers), he can first execute a complete circle (generally by age three), then a square (by age four), and then a triangle and cross (by six-and-a-half or seven). The four-year-old learns to print by drawing letters haphazardly all over the page, with letters even on their sides or backwards. The five-year-old should be able to begin to print his first name. The six-year-old will progress rapidly and should be able to print the alphabet, his first and last names, and the numbers one through ten (Cratty 1970). If you want to teach your child how to print, use both upper- and lower-case letters, because those are the letters he will learn in school for both printing and reading. If a child is taught to write a name in capital letters only, then he must unlearn that pattern and relearn capitals and lower-case letters when he gets into school. You are probably concerned about whether your child will write with his left or right hand; the section in this chapter on bilateral development discusses this topic.

Common Variations in Development Patterns

Small-muscle development will occur more slowly than large-muscle development—especially in boys.

Parents should strive to provide fun, interesting, and challenging fine motor opportunities. Boys who seem to show little interest in cutting and pasting may show great enthusiasm when pictures of animals or trucks are included. Preparing food involves small muscles; so does woodworking. Both boys and girls enjoy these activities. Many children rapidly overcome small-muscle deficiencies once they are motivated and have opportunities for practice. The parents' role is critical, since a child who enters kindergarten with few or no fine motor skills will be at a disadvantage.

Activities for Small-Muscle Development (Fine Motor Skills)

Small-muscle development is often neglected, but when its importance in daily living is considered, special emphasis should be given it.

Following is a list of suggested activities that will develop small muscles and will give your preschooler many opportunities for exploration, practice, and satisfaction. You will need to do some preparation, but include the child as much as possible in the preparation, use, and replacement of whatever you need for the activities. Your involvement will be exciting and enjoyable for both you and your child.

Your child can do many of the following activities unassisted:

Activities Using Household Items

Make containers: six-ounce cans for crayons, chalk, and paint brushes; egg cartons for sorting or holding scissors; baby food jars for paste and paint; three-pound shortening cans with plastic lids for clay, collage materials, and small toys; tissue boxes for collage materials or writing implements; cigar boxes, egg carton tops, shoebox lids, and small and large plastic or metal containers for numerous uses.

Tear paper (newspaper or tissue is easy) into large strips, tiny pieces, or various shapes.

Unscrew jars and lids, unscrew plastic nuts and bolts.

Turn pages of catalogs, books, and calendars.

Wind yarn or string onto spools (later, use thread).

Use kitchen utensils (knife, peeler, grater, scraper, or brush).

Clip clothespins on a box or line.

Sort nails, cans, or even buttons by color or composition (wood, plastic).

Fold napkins, paper or fabric; fold clothes; make paper hats, airplanes, or pinwheels; wrap packages.

Roll dough with hands or a rolling pin; roll socks together; crush crumbs; roll own body on floor; roll balls, marbles, or wheel toys.

Cut or tear pictures from old magazines.

Dress up in hats, shoes, bags, jewelry, clothes, and other props.

Match lids to various containers (use screw tops, corks, caps, plastic lids, and so on) and practice putting them on and taking them off.

Manipulate and make designs with one size of metal rings. Then introduce another size so the child can notice, compare, and make new designs. Later add a third size for noticing, comparing, and designing.

Use popsicle sticks or toothpicks in combination with various sized rings to make designs or collages.

Pick up various objects with tongs. Reduce the size of the tongs and objects as the child develops proficiency until he can pick up small objects (cereal, beads, buttons, and so on) with tweezers.

Make different shapes on newspaper (circle, triangle, squares, and so on) and then let the child cut the shapes out and color them with paint, marking pens, or large crayons. Or let him color inside the shapes and you cut them out. (Remember that the coloring may be crude.)

Use tweezers to dip cotton balls into paint and make designs.

Play the piano.

Use simple grooming implements: toothbrush, nail and hand brush, comb, and hairbrush.

Creative and Artistic Activities which Increase Fine Motor Skills
(Display all of your child's work with pride.)

Play with small blocks of different sizes, shapes, weights, and colors.

Model dough and clay (see recipes).

Fingerpaint (see recipes).

Cut and paste, either as an individual or combined activity. Start with simple designs and activities and move to more complex ones.

Make a collage from a variety of materials. As your child matures, expect him to use color, design, and materials in more sophisticated ways.

Draw a design on a piece of paper, then let your child lay toothpicks, popsicle sticks, or other objects over the shape. As your child matures, you could (1) draw a design for him to cover with sticks, (2) tell a simple story and have your child make stick figures to represent different people or objects, (3) give suggestions for stick building (Christmas and apple trees or animals such as dogs and birds), (4) help child make letters and numbers, (5) help child make designs representing parts of his environment, such as windows, doors, a church, fence, stairs, boats, hats, ladders, umbrellas, beds, chairs, tools, stars, or buildings.

Make a design with colored toothpicks on a table, on paper, or pressed into clay.

Make a design using gummed shapes, labels, or pictures.

Attach different-sized small wheels (from toy cars, trains, and so on) to a wire handle so that the wheels turn around. Dip the wheels into paint and make designs on paper, cardboard, or wood.

Make an easel using paper- or plastic-covered cardboard leaning on a chair back. Let your child mix and use paint with brushes on large sheets of paper.

Dip colored chalk into buttermilk or water. Draw on paper.

Partially cook some spaghetti and let your child arrange it on a piece of butcher or construction paper. It will stick to the paper when dry.

Paint, draw, or color. (Paint gives more freedom of movement than do crayons.) You provide the blank paper; the child does the creating.

Print on paper or cardboard with cork, a fork, a straw, or a potato dipped into thick poster paint.

Clap hands to various rhythms.

Make and use simple musical instruments from tubes, boxes, containers, or household items such as lids, pans, or spoons.

Save the cardboard from shirts, the paper cups from candy boxes, the aluminum pans from frozen foods and dinners, the tissues and packing from packages, and other such items for the child's fun and creative uses.

Activities Using Writing Utensils

Draw a maze, and then draw a path through the maze and let the child follow the path. If a plastic cover is placed over the drawing of the maze, different paths can be drawn over the maze with a grease pencil.

Connect dots color to color or shape to shape. Numbered dots are generally too advanced for a preschool child.

Draw horizontal and vertical lines over predrawn designs of a fence, house, bridge, road, or animal.

Trace dotted lines.

With his fingers, have your child trace shapes (circles, squares, triangles, ovals, stars, and so on) made of wood, heavy paper, or cardboard.

Complete figures or designs over partial drawings.

Trace shapes cut out of plastic or heavy cardboard with writing utensils, fingerpaint, sandpaper, and so on.

Have your child watch you print his name: Mary, not MARY; Robert, not ROBERT. Let your child copy what you have written if he is interested.

Stringing or Threading Activities

String beads, rigatoni, colored paper, straws, and so on.

Make sewing cards for your children. Paste a large picture on a piece of stiff cardboard and punch holes around the picture. Give your child a shoelace and let him "sew." The child could make valentines, cards, or ornaments.

Make a shoe out of a paper plate (see sample). The child laces through the eyelets.

Place beads of a certain color or shape on a dowel held in the other hand or held by another person.

Teach your child spool and hook "knitting" (see sample).

Make a simple macramé or practice tying (for a child who is ready).

Thread straws, shoe eyelets, spools, or buttons.

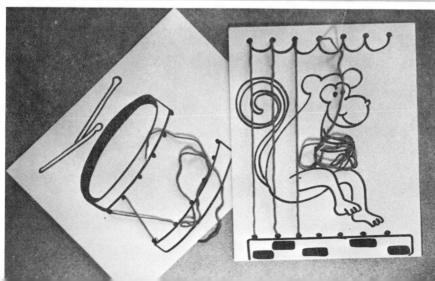

Use a large needle and colored yarn to sew on soft burlap. As a child's muscles develop, more experiences should be given—use smaller needles, provide large buttons to sew on, and so on.

Weave or interlace popsicle sticks, paper, yarn, rags, long grass, or straw to make simple placemats, hotpads, wall decorations, baskets, or other objects.

Dressing Activities

Dramatize housework and other grownup activities using dolls, clothing, furniture, and utensils.

Practice buttoning, snapping, zipping, hooking, and lacing on clothing or dressing frames (see sample).

Dress and undress dolls.

Cooking and Eating Activities

Provide finger foods for your child at meals and for snacks.

Set and clear the table.

Provide experiences for your child in breaking and cracking (eggs), chipping (ice), cutting and slicing, peeling, brushing, snapping (beans), shelling (peas), dipping, grating (cheese and vegetables), grinding (bread crumbs, meat, vegetables), measuring and leveling, stirring and mixing, pouring, pressing and shaping (cookie dough, meat balls), rolling (cookies, crumbs), spreading (butter, sandwiches, icing), whipping, and so on.

Put food or beverages in small containers and let your child serve himself. (Consumption is usually increased.)

Sprout and eat seeds.

Decorate cookies or cupcakes.

Sorting Activities

Sort playing cards into different piles according to color, suit, or number.

Sort bottle caps by color or kind into cups of an egg carton.

Sort buttons by size, color, composition (metal, glass, or plastic), or number of holes.

Sort small plastic chips (tiddly-winks or poker chips) by color.

Help your child color the cups of an egg carton. The child then picks up items of like colors and places them in the correct cup.

Pinching or Squeezing Activities

Play a simplified version of checkers. (The child helps make up the rules.)

Place various objects into large and small containers.

Place pegs into a pegboard.

Pinch clay, crepe paper, or cereal; wrap small objects; pick up matchsticks or toothpicks; clip clothespins on a box or line.

Squeeze icing through a tube, squeeze paste for pictures, squeeze toothpaste for brushing, or squeeze paint or water from catsup or

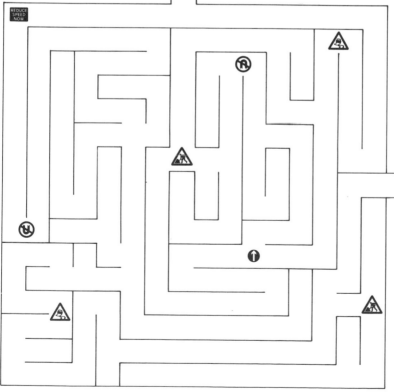

mustard dispensers; squeeze a rubber bulb to produce an air current and blow a sailboat or pinwheel; squeeze a rubber or plastic toy with a squeaker; squeeze art materials (clay, mud).

Make orange or lemon juice by squeezing with hand, juicer, or squeezer.

Operate a water pistol aimed at a target.

Pull weeds.

Provide eye-droppers, food coloring, and small containers (egg cartons, baby food jars) for child to practice mixing colors.

Activities for Manipulating or Finger Opposition

Pick up different objects (chunk cereal, coins, different sizes of yarn or string, buttons, eating utensils, and so on) with the thumb opposing each of the other four fingers separately.

With different-sized holes in a plastic carton or other containers, have your child place objects through correct-sized holes (pennies in a bank, cereal in a box, buttons in a can, beans through a slit in the top of an egg carton, tiddly-winks or poker chips through slits in milk or cottage cheese cartons, matchsticks or toothpicks through one-fourth-inch perforations, shoelaces through eyelets in shoes, needle and yarn through punched holes in heavy paper or cardboard).

Arrange flat popsicle sticks into designs or objects.

Play in different media (sand, dirt, flour, or cornmeal) with measuring cups and spoons or scoops.

Play in water with containers, floating objects, and various absorbing and nonabsorbing textures (plastic, fabric). Your child should try washing, squeezing, and wringing.

Play with rubber or wooden figures.

Stack and play with nesting blocks, cans, books, and cartons in various shapes, colors, and sizes.

Play with toy vehicles (trucks, trains, cars) on the table or floor.

Use small but sturdy tools (screwdriver, hammer, pliers).

Do simple puzzles (homemade or commercial).

Place various shapes over similar predrawn shapes on paper or cutout forms.

Construct items out of wood using woodworking tools or glue.

Practice pushing keys on an old typewriter.

Handle and use small balls, bean bags, marbles, and other materials for tossing, rolling, stacking, and bouncing.

Use push-pull floor or table toys.

Use hand, sock, and finger puppets.

Build with materials similar to Tinker Toys, Lincoln Logs, Lego, Multi-fit.

Experiment with good, workable scissors and easy-to-cut materials.

Let your child cut at will, or make some simple designs for your child. (To cut out a square, use long, continuous cuts; to cut a circle, use smaller, smoother cuts; to cut a pine tree design, use short, individual cuts.) You can show your child how to hold the scissors and how to cut; however, he may be more interested in simply working

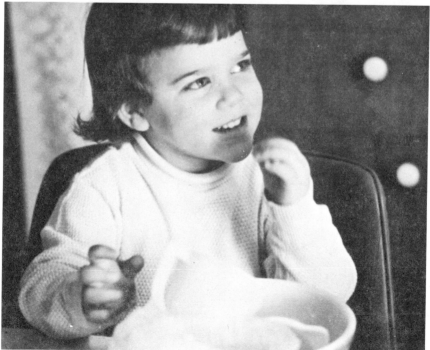

the scissors than in following any specific design.

Use art materials—especially brushes (paste and paint), large crayons, and good tools.

Do fun hand games, fingerplays, counting games, and songs.

Have sensory or "feeling" opportunities—provide your child with a variety of textures, temperatures, and objects from nature (rocks, shells, leaves, animal coverings).

Make shapes out of yarn or string laid on the table or floor.

Make felt or sandpaper letters and numbers for the child to trace with his fingers.

Make a texture cube for the child with different texture on each side.

Plant seeds in pots or containers.

Make a gadget board for the child to use.

Left-Right (Bilateral) Development

Handedness

You are probably concerned whether your child will be right- or left-handed. There are two philosophies regarding handedness. The first is that eye, hand, and foot preferences seem to be determined by heredity but that they are influenced by pressures from society and culture (Cratty 1970). The other view, which seems to be based on strong evidence, is that handedness is a learned skill. However, both views indicate that forcing a child to change from the left to the right hand could cause problems such as resistance, confusion, and tension.

It is better for a child to remain left-handed (if that pattern is firmly established) than for his development to be disrupted. If handedness is not firmly established, it can be changed under these favorable conditions: (1) if the child is under six years of age; (2) if he uses both hands interchangeably; (3) if no permanent difficulty arises after a trial period; (4) if the change is agreeable to the child; and (5) if he is above average in intelligence (Hildreth 1950). More important than *which* hand the child uses is *how well* he can use the hands as tools in learning.

The years between two and five see hand preference firmly established in most children, indicating that it is a trait of development which increases with maturity but which is influenced by both heredity and social learning. It is interesting to note that boys seem to show a greater incidence of left-handedness and ambidexterity. If a child shows a strong preference for the left hand, it is wise to give him left-handed equipment (tools, scissors) when possible and also to show him how to adapt to right-handed tools and arrangements.

Discrimination Between Left and Right

Another, even more important, part of bilateral development is learning to distinguish left from right. Even though the child can't identify left and right hands with any accuracy until he is six or seven years of age, some of his later learning may depend on left-right discriminations that are related to his body and to orientations in space (such as directions in a task or community). Some researchers have designed specific programs to help children make left-right body discriminations, believed to prevent later reading and learning problems such as difficulty in telling p from q, b from d, and so on. (Cratty 1970.) Because a child learns better when he is not frustrated or pressured, it seems wise to evaluate such programs thoroughly.

Activities for Bilateral (Left-Right) Development

You can give your child many good experiences to help him make left-right distinctions without making the process painful or compulsory. Following are some suggestions, and you can probably come up with others that may be more meaningful for your own child.

It is possible for a five-year-old to learn that there are left and right parts of his body and of other things, but accurate left-right abilities are not developed much before the age of seven. The following activities will give the child experience with the words *left* and *right* and with orientation of his body to these words. You should not attempt to "teach" left and right to the child; participation should be encouraged in a warm, friendly atmosphere without any expected level of performance. Make sure your child knows the difference between *right* as the opposite of *left* and *right* as the opposite of *wrong*. If you don't help make this distinction, he could get confused.

Try to stand or sit next to the child when showing him left and right, so that his right is on the same side as yours. If you are facing the child, hold up your left hand (as a mirror image) when identifying his right hand.

Put a colored ribbon or bracelet on the right hand and right leg or left hand and left leg, but only emphasize one side at a time. Label (say "right" or "left") for the child. Do activities throughout the day that emphasize the same side of the body.

Label right and left as the child performs daily activities. Instruct the child to "put your right arm in the right sleeve," or "tie your right shoe" (if the child is able to tie shoes). Dwell on *right* until it is learned. Then introduce left, and later work with a combination of the two.

After extended experience with the above activities, put a different-colored ribbon on your child's right and left legs. Ask your child to step on like-colored objects with the correct leg (for example, if the child has a red ribbon on his left leg, he should step only on red-colored objects with that leg).

Play a modified version of the "Twister Game." At first use only colors or shapes: "Put your right foot on a circle." "Put your right foot on a square." Be careful not to introduce too many variables (colors, sizes, shapes, or sides of the body).

Make a horizontal design with beads on a string, train cars, blocks, or some other series of objects and ask your child to duplicate it. Be sure to form the design from the child's left to his right.

Play a game using right and left. A fun one is the "Hokey-Pokey" ("You put your right foot in, you put your right foot out . . .").

Show the child how to set the table with the forks on the left and the knives and spoons on the right.

Using a pencil flashlight on a page of a book or a large flashlight on a wall or flannel board, show the child the left-right sequence used in reading and writing. Start the light at the left of the paper and move it slowly to the right. Turn it off at the end of each line. Then focus on the left side and turn the light back on. (Or use your finger to follow the words as you read a story to the child.)

Make up opportunities to show the child the left to right sequencing.

Do fingerplays involving numbers ("Ten Little Indians," "Five Little Ducks," and so on). As numbers are said, always raise fingers from left to right for the child.

Help your child learn motor skills: skip (step on right foot and hop, then step on left foot and hop), throw a ball (step on one foot and throw with the opposite hand), march (swing the opposite arm with each step), run, climb (use an opposite hand and foot motion), ride or pedal a tricycle or toy car (push first with one foot and then with the other).

Always start in the upper left-hand corner when writing the child's name on paper, and always begin horizontal lines at the left and vertical lines at the top left.

Do songs and fingerplays involving left and right:

My Right Hand

This is my right hand.   (Extend it.)
I raise it up high.   (Raise it.)
This is my left hand.   (Extend it.)
I will touch the sky.   (Raise it.)
Right hand, left hand.   (Show each.)
Whirl them around.   (Do it.)
Right hand, left hand.   (Show each.)
Pound, pound, pound.   (Do it.)
[Anonymous]

Mr. Left and Mr. Right

This is Mr. Left. (Hold up left thumb.)
This is Mr. Right. (Hold up right thumb.)
Mr. Left lives in a house (make a fist for the house) at the top of a hill. He opens the door (fingers out) and goes inside (thumb goes into opened fist). He closes the door (fingers close).
Mr. Right lives in another house (other fist) at the top of another hill. He opens the door (fingers out) and goes inside (thumb into opened fist). He closes the door (fingers close).
One day Mr. Left opened his door and came out of his house (thumb comes out of fist). He closed the door and said, "It's such a nice day. I think I'll go for a walk and visit my friend, Mr. Right."
Mr. Left walked down the hill, and up a hill, down another hill and up

a hill. (Pantomime the up-and-down walk.) He came to Mr. Right's house. He knocked on the door (left fist knocks on right fist), waited a few seconds, and knocked again. "I guess Mr. Right is not home. I'll come back another day."

Mr. Left walked back down the hill, up the other hill, down the hill, and up the hill to his own house. He opened the door, went inside, and closed the door.

(Repeat for Mr. Right.)

Another day they decided to visit each other.

They opened their doors, stepped outside and closed their doors.

They both walked down the hill and up the hill until they met.

"How do you do, Mr. Right," said Mr. Left.

"How do you do, Mr. Left," said Mr. Right.

They talked and talked and talked (wiggle thumbs). When the sun was low in the west, they each waved "Good-bye." Then each went down the hill, and up the hill back to his own house. They popped into their houses, and were out of sight. (Pantomime with thumbs. End with thumbs inside fists.)

(Todd, V. E., and G. H. Hunter, *The Aide in Early Childhood Education* [New York: the Macmillan Company, 1973], pp. 203–204. Used by permission of Macmillan Company.)

Food and Nutrition

Importance of Good Nutrition

Your child's physical growth depends directly on both his own nutrition and the mother's nutrition before and during pregnancy. Poor nutrition can cause severely stunted growth, and when children are smaller in stature or lighter in weight than average, nutritional rather than racial or genetic factors are usually responsible (Smart and Smart 1973). Depressed learning capacity is also definitely associated with

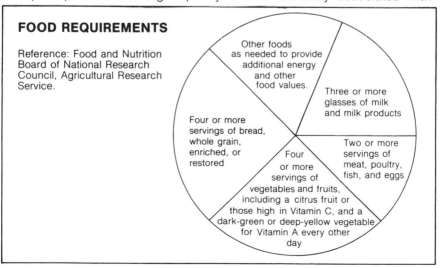

FOOD REQUIREMENTS

Reference: Food and Nutrition Board of National Research Council, Agricultural Research Service.

Other foods as needed to provide additional energy and other food values.

Three or more glasses of milk and milk products

Two or more servings of meat, poultry, fish, and eggs

Four or more servings of vegetables and fruits, including a citrus fruit or those high in Vitamin C, and a dark-green or deep-yellow vegetable for Vitamin A every other day

Four or more servings of bread, whole grain, enriched, or restored poor nourishment; in addition, a child's resistance to disease is lowered, his defects are emphasized, his energy is lacking, his self-image is negative, and he is unappealing to others. With all of these physical strikes against the child, his chances of academic survival are small.

Periods of Nutrition Critical to Good Growth

The mother's pregnancy is a vital period. The more healthy and better cared for she is during her pregnancy, the better the mother's chances are of giving her child a strong, healthy body. If a pregnant woman has a poor diet, abuses drugs, drinks large amounts of alcohol, smokes cigarettes, has a viral illness (smallpox, mumps, scarlet fever, chicken pox, or German measles) during the first three months, or is exposed to radiation (x-rays), there is a good chance that her offspring will be premature, will die soon after birth, or will have some kind of birth defect (Lugo and Hershey 1974).

It is critical that a young child receive nourishing food. If a child is half-starved during the first six months of his life, he may be permanently stunted; but if starvation occurs after the age of two, the child will probably recover (Brophy 1975). Nourishing foods are essential for good physical development of the total body, including muscles, sensory perceptors, bones, organs, and the brain. If you stop to think that ninety percent of a person's brain growth is achieved by the age of six years, you will realize how important good nutrition is for cognitive development alone (Brophy 1975).

The following daily food requirements are recommended for preschool children by the Agricultural Research Service:

Three or more cups of milk and milk products

Two or more servings of meat, poultry, fish, and eggs

Four or more servings of vegetables and fruits, including a citrus fruit or other fruit or vegetable high in vitamin C daily and a dark-green or deep-yellow vegetable for vitamin A at least every other day

Four or more servings of bread and cereal of whole grain, enriched, or restored variety

Other foods as needed to provide additional energy and other food values

Figures are not to be taken completely literally. Individuals vary in the amounts they need and in the amounts they eat from one day to another and from one meal to another. If the foods offered are chosen along the lines of this plan, most preschool children will receive the nutritional elements they need.

Physical Characteristics Influenced by Feeding Habits

The child will depend on you to provide growth-promoting and protective foods; it is your responsibility to provide ample good foods that will give physical stamina and promote healthy growth and to minimize "junk" foods with empty calories but no proteins, minerals, or vitamins.

Because the preschooler has only half the stomach capacity that an adult has, he may not be able to eat as much as you expect. The stomach also readily empties in either direction because its alignment is straighter and more directly upright than a younger or older child's.

During the preschool years, the child requires only slightly more than half the caloric intake of an active adult. Since a child's appetite is easily dulled by eating sweets before a meal, you should be firm in refusing his requests for candy, cookies, or ice cream: eating them will prevent your child from getting the food he needs for physical growth and will expose him to tooth decay. There is also a suspected relationship between sweets and hyperactivity in children.

If you are careful about your child's eating habits between the ages of two and three, many food problems can be eliminated. Up until two, growth is quite rapid and a child needs lots of food to "stoke the engine." As your child approaches three, his intake decreases because of slower growth; the decrease is due to a change in growth, and is generally not a result of illness or crankiness. Also at about the age of three your child will show more independence by demanding or refusing certain foods, and your urging or forcing food will only cause more resistance. You will help your child develop good eating habits by offering him a variety of foods.

The preschooler's mouth is also different from yours—just like his stomach. His mouth lining is very tender, and your child may forget that food may be too hot; you will need to check the temperature of food carefully.

The child's digestive tract is easily irritated by seasonings and roughage, and because his taste buds are more keen than those of older children and adults, foods should be seasoned less and should be unmixed (limit the number of casseroles and stews). Keep the food rather bland and let other family members season it to their liking. The preschooler likes to hold food in his cheeks because he wants to savor the flavor against his taste buds.

Emotional Aspects of Feeding

During infancy, you fed your child whenever he cried, thus developing your child's sense of trust in you and in the world. Now that your child is of preschool age, he will benefit more from a meal schedule based on the stage of his maturity—he generally needs three meals per day plus a nourishing snack both in the morning and the afternoon. If your preschooler comes to meals ravenously hungry or completely exhausted, he probably won't eat much. One mother recognized signs of extreme hunger in her child, so, upon such occasions, she would give the child several ounces of juice or milk, one soda cracker, *or* a few pieces of raw fruit or vegetables about a half-hour prior to the meal. The child's behavior changed so that he enjoyed the following meal. Another mother perceived that fatigue caused her daughter to become irritable and refuse meals. This was a sign for the mother to clear her commitments to everything but the child and the two of them would enjoy a book, a record, or a conversation together. The little girl's appetite recovered under this calming atmosphere.

The preschooler is an inexperienced snack or meal planner, so don't ask him what he would like to eat, and don't give him an unlimited choice. If you do, he will probably ask for foods that are high in carbohydrates and fats (cookies, candy, gum, or potato chips). Instead, offer limited alternatives among nourishing foods that contain proteins, minerals, and vitamins (milk, eggs, cheese, raw fruits and vegetables, or juices). Whenever possible, let the child make his own choice between two alternative foods, both acceptable to you. Even better, allow the child to serve himself and then eat what's on his plate. It is very satisfying for the child to be responsible for his own food intake; occasionally you may need to caution him about amounts, but don't punish your child by making him sit at the table until he finishes an unreasonable amount of food just because he used poor judgment in dishing it up.

Your preschooler can also develop autonomy by pouring his own beverage if you put it in a small cream or syrup pitcher. Usually the child will drink more, too, if he can pour the drink himself. Offer your child milk, juice, and other liquids several times each day, because it is easy for a young child to become dehydrated.

When introducing new foods (it isn't wise to do this more than once a week), put a small amount on your child's plate or—better still—let him dish up a small serving himself and examine it. Your child may not eat it the first time or two, but offer it to him anyway. When the food is more familiar, your child will feel better about trying it. How often have you seen a young child try a new food, pull a distorted face, and then remove the food from his mouth with his hands—or just spit it out? The taste, the texture, the temperature, or something else about the food is distasteful. Later on, the child may develop a liking for that food, but if you force the child to eat it, you're both in for an unhappy power struggle and other new foods may not be well accepted later on.

Food that looks attractive on the plate and that has a variety of colors and textures is more fun for your child to eat. Mashed potatoes, cauliflower, white fish in a white sauce, peeled apple slices, and vanilla pudding would not be nearly as appealing and colorful as baked potato, peas, fried fish, carrot sticks, and a fruit cup.

Foods that can be picked up with the fingers (raw fruits and vegetables, bread, and meat strips) are easier to handle, since eating with utensils is still pretty new and difficult for the child. Children usually like raw fruit and vegetables because they are crispy and crunchy and make the child feel powerful when his teeth snap and chew. Some children object to different textures: introduce gradually foods that are gritty, pulpy (some thick juices like apricot or tomato), and stringy (beans, squash).

If you see the child sorting out the vegetables in your famous stew or picking out the ingredients of your prize-winning casserole, it's not that he is finicky. Most preschool children like their foods separate so that they can really taste and enjoy their uniqueness (potatoes here, peas there, carrots over there, meat here). Later on your child will really go for your casseroles and mixed dishes.

Whenever possible, let the child eat with you and the rest of the family. Engage in delightful nonemotional conversation as you enjoy each other and your food. When mealtime becomes stressful, no one eats and digests food properly. Food is rapidly consumed, unenjoyed, and unappreciated. If hunger wasn't such an uncomfortable feeling, one would just as soon skip the whole meal.

Don't be upset if your child puts his hands in the plate. Children of this age are very proud of what their fingers can do, and fingers seem so much more dependable now than do a spoon or fork. When the gelatin wiggles or the peas roll or the ice cream slides, the child can learn a lot more about those foods by *feeling* them with his hands than he can by holding them in a spoon. Your child isn't asking you to be tolerant of inappropriate or disgusting behavior; instead, try to understand and help him to do better. The preschooler wants to develop good eating habits and good table manners; you can help by providing a good, noncritical model. If the child can see what you expect, he will try to please you by acting the way you do.

If your preschooler spills or makes a mess (tips over the milk or slides food off the plate), let him wipe it up (with your help, if necessary) without you displaying any anger or emotional outbursts. The more calmly both of you respond, the more you benefit from increased goodwill and pleasant mealtimes. The child who hears, "It's all right. Get the sponge and wipe it up before it runs onto the floor," can accept his inabilities much better than a child who hears his parent scream, "I knew you'd spill if I let you do it. Can't you ever do anything right?" Commend him for his good performances at meals. It will help show your confidence and respect in him.

Activities to Develop Awareness of Food and Nutrition

Nutrition, eating, and growing are all important parts of the child's development. Try looking at them from his point of view often and you'll both get along just fine.

There are many ways you can help your child become conscious of eating good foods. Look over the following activities—then do them together or begin your own collection. Food experiences like these can bring you and your child closer together.

One of the best ways to interest a child in food and eating is to involve him in the selection and preparation of food. If he can help decide what to have, judge good quality, and prepare and serve it, he has a vested interest in food. Generally children try new foods, enjoy eating, and eat more when they have been involved.

Food preparation
See cooking suggestions under "Activities for Small-Muscle Development (Fine Motor Skills)."
A preschool child can do many things related to food. He can butter bread or toast for himself or the family, assist in preparing for a picnic or making sandwiches, wash and brush vegetables, remove

stems from fruit (cherries and grapes), decorate cookies and cup-cakes, shell peas, assist in making applesauce (peeling and stir-ring), make his own loaf of bread or a pie, whip instant puddings, make gelatin, cut fruit to make a salad, prepare a beverage, and many more.

Other Activities

Let your child assist you in checking your supplies and making a shopping list.

Let your child arrange food on the shelves (by pictures on cans).

Eat in a different location (outside or at the park).

Let your child invite a guest for lunch occasionally.

If you have a small plot of ground, grow a garden or provide a space where the child can grow a garden of his own. Get seeds that germinate rapidly, like radishes or beans. If you have no outside area, grow tomatoes in a container, get seed strips, sprout and eat seeds, grow herbs in small containers, or plant strawberries in a barrel. Let the child help prepare the soil, plant the seeds, care for the plants, and harvest the produce.

Take the child to the market and show him how you select your pro-duce. Even if you don't buy all the items, tell him what they are and how they are eaten (raw, cooked, in salads, and so on). Try some new ones that your child picks out.

Tell your child how you decide on the quantity to buy.

Show your child how food is sold (by the pound, dozen, basket, bushel, can, or case).

Show your child how food is stored (frozen, dried, or canned).

Make a chart of the basic four food groups. Let your child check off what he eats in each food group each day.

Give your child a separate sheet of paper for each of the four food groups. Let him go through an old magazine and cut out pictures for each group and then paste them into a booklet. (The booklet may be expanded over a period of time.)

Help your child exercise his senses of autonomy and independence by letting him occasionally prepare and serve the food and clear the table.

Compliment your child on his contributions to the meal.

Let your child examine and play with plastic replicas of fruit and veg-etables.

Show your child how one fruit or vegetable can be served in many different ways; for instance, an apple can be eaten raw or made into juice, applesauce, pie, or jam, or it can be dried.

Show your child the different parts of plants that are edible, such as the root of the carrot, the stalk of the celery, the leaf of the let-tuce, and the blossom of the cauliflower.

Take your child to various places in the community where food is ob-tained (the bakery, butcher shop, orchard, poultry farm, dairy, fish hatchery, or restaurant).

Make fruit leather with your child (see the recipe section).

Children's Books on the Body and Its Skills, Food, and Nutrition

Aliki, *My Five Senses,* Thos. Y. Crowell, 1962.

Aliki, *My Hands.*

Balestrino, Phillip, *The Skeleton Inside You,* Thos. Y. Crowell.

Becky, *Tall Enough Tommy,* Children's Press, 1946.

Berg, Jean H., *Baby Susan's Chickens,* Wonder Books, 1951.

Bond, Gladys B., *Patrick Will Grow,* Whitman, 1966.

Collier, Ethel, *Who Goes There in My Garden?,* Young Scott, 1963.

Cook, Bernadine, *The Little Fish that Got Away,* Young Scott.

Crume, Marion, *Let Me See You Try,* Glendale, Calif.: Bowmar, 1970.

Darby, Gene, *What Is a Plant?,* Benefic Press, 1958.

Darby, Gene, *What Is a Chicken?,* Benefic Press, 1958.

Darby, Gene, *What Is a Cow?,* Benefic Press, 1963.

Darby, Gene, *What Is a Fish?,* Benefic Press, 1958.

Green, Carla, *I Want to Be a Fisherman,* Children's Press.

Green, Mary M., *Is It Hard? Is It Easy?,* Wm. R. Scott, 1960.

Green, Mary, M., *Everybody Eats,* Wm. R. Scott, 1950.

Huntington, Harriet E., *Let's Go Outdoors,* Doubleday, 1939.

Ivens, Dorothy, *The Long Hike,* Viking Press, 1956.

Jaynes, Ruth M., *Watch Me Outdoors,* Glendale, Calif.: Bowmar, 1967.

Jaynes, Ruth M., *My Tricycle and I,* Glendale, Calif.: Bowmar, 1968.

Jordan, Helene J., *Seeds by Wind and Water,* Thos. Y. Crowell, 1962.

Jordan, Helene J., *How a Seed Grows,* Thos. Y. Crowell.

Krauss, Ruth, *The Carrot Seed,* Harper and Bros., 1945.

Krauss, Ruth, *The Growing Story,* Harper and Bros., 1947.

Lenski, Lois, *"Small" series,* Henry Walck.

Martin, Dick, *The Apple Book,* Golden Press, 1964.

Martin, Dick, *The Fish Book,* Golden Press, 1964.

McCloskey, Robert, *Blueberries for Sal,* Viking Press, 1966.

Rice, Inez, *A Long, Long Time,* Lothrop, Lee, and Shepard, 1964.

Rothschild, Alice, *Fruit Is Ripe for Timothy,* Young Scott, 1963.

Selsam, Millicent E., *Seeds and More Seeds,* Harper and Bros., 1959.

Selsam, Millicent E., *The Plants We Eat,* Wm. Morrow and Co., 1965.

Smith, Laura and Ernie, *Things That Grow,* Melmont, 1958.

Steiner, Charlotte, *"Kiki" series,* Doubleday.

Webber, Irma E., *Bits That Grow Big,* Wm. R. Scott, 1959.

Webber, Irma E., *Up Above and Down Below,* Wm. R. Scott, 1943.

Wright, Ethel, *Saturday Ride,* Wm. R. Scott, 1952.

Wright, Ethel, *Saturday Walk,* Wm. R. Scott, 1951.

Young, Edward W., *Norman and the Nursery School,* Platt and Munk, 1959.

References for Adults

Belgau, F., *A Motor Perceptual Development Handbook of Activities for Schools, Parents and Preschool Programs,* La Porte, Texas: Perception Development Research Assoc., 1967.

Borsen, Minnie, *Opening, Mixing, Matching,* Washington, D.C.: Assoc. for Childhood International, 1974.

Breckenridge, M. E., and M. N. Murphy, *Growth and Development of the Young Child,* eighth edition, Philadelphia: Saunders, 1969.

Cratty, Bryant J., *Perceptual and Motor Development in Infants and Children,* New York: Macmillan Company, 1970.

Cratty, B. J., *Intelligence in Action: Physical Activities for Enhancing Intellectual Abilities,* Englewood Cliffs, N.J.: Prentice-Hall, Inc., 1973.

DeHirsch, K., J. Jansky, and W. Langford, *Predicting Reading Failure,* New York: Harper and Row, 1966.

Dierks, E. C., and L. M. Morse, "Good Habits and Nutrient Intakes of Preschool Children," *J. Am. Dietetics Assoc.* 47 (1965), 292–296.

Eichenwald, H., and P. Fry, "Nutrition and Learning," *Science* 163 (1969), 644–48.

Erickson, Eric, *A Health Personality for Your Child,* Washington, D.C.: Superintendent of Documents, Result of Midcentury White House Conference on Children and Youth, December 1950.

Frank, Lawrence K., "Tactile Communication," in C. B. Kopp, editor, *Readings in Early Development: for Occupational and Physical Therapy Students,* Springfield, Ill.: Charles C. Thomas, publisher, 1971.

Frostig, M. and D. Horne, *The Frostig Program for the Development of Visual Perception,* Chicago: Follett, 1964.

Gerhardt, Lydia, *Moving and Knowing: The Young Child Orients Himself in Space,* Englewood Cliffs, N.J.: Prentice-Hall, 1973.

Gesell, A., H. M. Halverson, H. Thompson, and F. Ilg, *The First Five Years of Life: A Guide to the Study of the Preschool Child,* New York: Harper and Row, 1940.

Guilford, J. P., "A System of Psychomotor Abilities," *American Journal of Psychology* 71 (1958), 146–147.

Hendrick, Joanne, *The Whole Child: New Trends in Early Education,* St. Louis: the C.V. Mosby Company, 1975.

Hildreth, G., "The Development of Training of Hand Dominance," *J. Genet. Psychol.* 75 (1950), 197–220; 76 (1951), 39–144.

Hodges, W. L., B. R. McCandless, H. H. Spicker, and I. S. Craig, *Diagnostic Teaching for Preschool Children,* Arlington, Va.: Council for Exceptional Children, 1971.

Hurlock, Elizabeth, *Child Development,* New York: McGraw-Hill, 1972.

Ilg, Frances L., and Louise B. Ames, *School Readiness: Behavior Tests Used at the Gesell Institute,* New York, Evanston and London: Harper and Row, 1965.

Kellogg, R., and S. O'Dell, *Analyzing Children's Art,* Palo Alto, Calif: National Press Books, 1969.

Laban, R., *The Mastery of Movement,* second edition, London: MacDonald and Evans, 1960.

Lazroe, J., "An Investigation of the Effects of Motor Training on the Reading Readiness of Kindergarten Children," *Dissertation Abstracts,* 29:8 (1969), 2609a.

Leithwood, K. A., and W. Fowler, "Complex Motor Learning in the Four-Year-Old," *Child Dev.* 42 (1971), 781–792.

Montagu, Ashley, *Touching: The Human Significance of the Skin,* New York: Columbia University Press, 1971.

Pederson, F. A., and P. H. Wender, "Early Social Correlates of Cognitive Functioning in Six-Year-Old Boys," *Child Dev.* 39 (1968), 185–193.

Sinclair, C. B., *Movement of the Young Child: Ages Two to Six,* Columbus, Ohio: Charles E. Merrill Publishing Company, 1973.

Smart, Mollie, and Russell C. Smart, *Preschool Children: Development and Relationships,* New York: Macmillan Company, 1973.

Smart, M. S., and R. C. Smart, *Child Development and Relationships,* second edition, New York: Macmillan Company, 1972.

Taylor, Barbara J., *A Child Goes Forth,* revised edition, Provo, Utah: Brigham Young University Press, 1975.

Taylor, Barbara J., *When I Do, I Learn,* Provo, Utah: Brigham Young University Press, 1974.

Todd, Vivian Edmiston, and Georgennie H. Hunter, *The Aide in Early Childhood Education,* New York: Macmillan Company, 1973.

Watson, E. H., and G. H. Lowrey, *Growth and Development of Children,* fifth edition, Chicago: Year Book, 1967.

Wickstrom, R. L., *Fundamental Motor Patterns,* Philadelphia: Lea and Febiger, 1970.

Two

Intellectual (Cognitive) Development

A Note from Your Preschooler

Dear Mom and Dad,

My mind grew yesterday—and so did my eyes and my ears and my nose and my tongue. You probably didn't see it happen, but it did.

I learn by feeling things with my fingers, by putting things in my mouth, by pushing and pulling them, by looking at them, by listening to them, and by smelling them. I want to see how things work, what I can do with them, and what they're made of.

I'm trying to learn to listen better and to talk better, too. I want you to help me get ready to learn to read.

I need to do things myself, and when I play it helps me learn things. I can't learn from books or TV very well yet.

I like thinking about what is happening right now, today. It's hard for me to think about yesterday and tomorrow.

I believe everything I see; and I can only see things from my viewpoint. Sometimes I like to fool you by pretending to be somebody else.

I'm learning to think faster and about more things. But sometimes what I want and what I see right now get in the way.

When something is too hard, my mind shuts off. Please don't show me how to do everything *your* way all the time. I need to be by myself and spend lots of time learning things *my* way.

I like numbers and letters. I have to ask lots of questions about them. Please help me learn to count, and please read to me lots.

I have to feel like you *love* me before I want to work hard and learn.

      Love,
      Your Preschooler

Introduction

Parents often hesitate to challenge their children intellectually, using the excuse that "I'm not trained to be a teacher," "That's the school's job," "I don't have time," or "I wouldn't know what to do."

Parents *are* teachers of their children at all times—whether or not they intend to be or want to be. Parents spend much more time with a child than a professional teacher does; parents see the child in many more circumstances than does the professional teacher. Who feeds the child when hunger sets in? Who stays up with the child during illness or upsets? Who is legally responsible for the total well-being of the child? If parents weren't so vitally important, society would have found a replacement for them long ago.

Some parents feel confident in their ability to meet the needs of their children; other parents want guidance and direction. All children want love from and interaction with their parents; many parents unknowingly do many good things to promote healthy intellectual growth in their children.

As a basic guideline to the preschoolers' intellectual development, most children of three years of age can point to and name some of the body parts, can match primary colors, and can name familiar animals. At four years of age they can count to five, can repeat four digits, can define objects in terms of their use, and can recognize the names of colors and shapes. At five years of age they can deal with simple opposites, can count to ten, can recognize coins, can name colors, and they have time concepts relating to the day and week. At six years of age they can repeat five digits, can give uses of some simple objects, can name at least five colors, can count to one hundred, and have concepts of time, space, number, and shape (Papalia and Olds 1975).

Activities to Stimulate Intellectual Development

Activities Using Pictures

Show your child pictures that demonstrate action (running, flying, and other activities). Have your child identify the action and then demonstrate it.

Show your child pictures of people, animals, or objects; let him tell what they do or say.

Assemble a series of pictures and have your child put them in proper sequence (child sleeping, waking, dressing, eating, playing).

Present to your child a picture of an entire animal (cow); cut the picture into various parts (head, tail, leg, udder) and put them into a sack or box. Let your child take the picture pieces out of the sack, tell what they are, and put the animal together like a puzzle. Have a similar activity with pictures of other familiar things (human, car, fruit, house, toy) that have only a few parts. Move to more parts and more complex pictures as the child indicates interest and ability.

Divide equal-sized pictures of two familiar animals into three parts— head, body, and tail. Give your child the six pieces and have him put them together to make two separate animals.

PRESCHOOLER'S INTELLECTUAL DEVELOPMENT

Age	Achievement
3	Can point to and name some body parts, can match primary colors, and can name familiar animals.
4	Can count to five, can repeat four digits, can define objects in terms of their use, and can recognize names of colors and shapes.
5	Can deal with simple opposites, can count to ten, can recognize coins and can name colors, and can understand time concepts relating to the day and the week.
6	Can repeat five digits, can give uses of some simple objects, can name at least five colors, can count to one hundred, and can have concepts of time, space, number, and shape.

Reference: Papalia and Olds, 1975

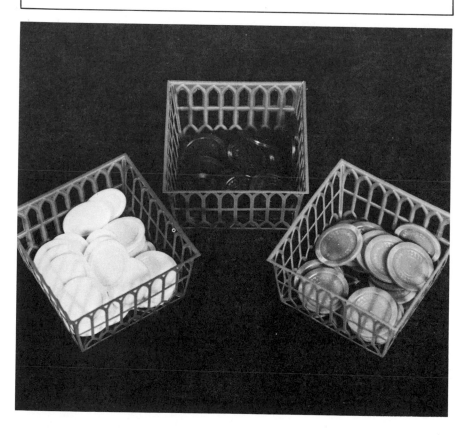

Find several pictures that illustrate one or the other of two opposing categories (zoo and farm animals, winter and summer activities, or day and night activities). With a string or yarn, divide a table or an area on the floor. Help your child put similar pictures together, occasionally discussing his reasoning.

Put a sheet of construction or heavy paper over a large (8½″ by 11″), simple picture. Make windows over strategic parts of the picture (such as the tail, wing, and propeller of an airplane or the stem, leaves, and blossoms of a plant) and then ask the child to open the windows one at a time and try to guess what the picture is. Once the child has opened all the windows, expose the whole picture and discuss it with your child.

Help your child match proper pairs of animal babies with mothers.

Help your child match animals and their homes.

Manipulative Activities

Cut or tear pictures that go together from magazines (food, body parts, clothes).

Compare sizes—objects, rooms and closet, animals, blocks, toys, measuring cups, balls, trees, cars.

Combine shapes after talking about the characteristics of each one.

Make play dough, clay, fingerpaints, and other art materials. Discuss the process. (See recipe section.)

Cut out circles from cardboard and put appropriate colors of cellophane or plastic over the openings to make a traffic signal light; discuss with your child the meaning of each light: red means stop, yellow means be careful or go slowly, green means go. Put a flashlight behind each circle to emphasize it for the child. Continue the discussion at a real traffic light.

Cut up a picture of a plant or a tree so that each part is separate. Let your child put them in order on a piece of paper, on the table, or on a flannel board. Try to show the seed, stem, leaves, and flower of a plant; roots, trunk, limb, branches, twigs, leaves, and blossoms of a tree.

Show your child three objects, then cover them with a cloth. Have your child close his eyes while you remove one object. See if he can remember which thing was removed.

Match things: (1) visible objects, such as buttons, animal stamps, Christmas stickers, simple picture dominoes, fabric swatches, and wallpaper samples; (2) tactile stimuli, such as sensory items, textures and thicknesses; (3) auditory stimuli, such as simple sounds, rhythms, and melodies; (4) tastes; (5) smells (look alikes, such as white substances—powdered and granulated sugar, baking powder, soap, and so on); and (6) actions: shadow and mirror dancing, follow-the-leader, Simon Says.

Play with nesting cubes (each cube fits into a slightly larger one).

Cut a large arrow out of poster board or wood and ask your child to point the arrow to different objects as you name them (door, ceiling, shelf). Then trade places with the child.

Play *object in motion* to help your child learn about prepositions: inside/outside, above/below, into/out of, in/out, empty/full, off/on, open/close, on top of/under, behind or in back of/in front of, stopped/moving.

Help your child learn one color, and then make a large circle (wheel) out of it. When your child has learned to identify that color, add another color to make a two-color wheel. Continue over a long period of time until there is a complete color wheel.

Make a color wheel for your child (the number of colors you use depends on his knowledge), and then provide small magazine pictures that are the same colors as those on the wheel. Let your child attach the pictures to the appropriate colors.

Help your child make an ant farm by putting dark paper around a jar, getting ants, and putting them into the jar. Place bread or cookie crumbs, honey, or sugar water inside the jar for the ants to eat. When the paper is removed, the ants will be near the glass.

Buy a pet for your child that he can care for—frog, ants, fish, bird, dog, or cat.

Help your child make a terrarium.

Provide junk materials for your child to use in making pictures (paper, fabrics, and so on).

Get an old paint sample book from the paint store and select two or three shades of the same color; let your child arrange them from light to dark or vice versa. As the colors are learned, add more shades and let your child arrange them.

Encourage your child to use his imagination with empty cartons and containers to build toys (egg carton: bus, caterpillar, basket; cardboard tubes: horns, wheels, telescope, towers).

Help your child make a bug catcher out of an old oatmeal or salt box. Put screen or mesh over the windows and make a handle of yarn. Help your child catch bugs.

Language Activities

Talk about time concepts—yesterday, today, tomorrow, tonight.

Discuss the proper care for plants or animals.

Discuss similarities with your child. Talk about likenesses of shape, color, size, and so on. Use the words *alike* and *different.*

Ask your child riddles, giving him as many clues as he needs to guess the answer. For example: (1) "I am thinking about something you wear on your foot. Some of them tie, some buckle, and some slip on. Can you guess?" (2) "I went to the farm and saw lots of animals. Let me tell you about them and see if you can guess what I saw. This animal has four legs and horns and gives milk. Can you guess?" "This one is harder. It has two legs, wings, and feathers."

(Your child may guess a chicken, turkey, bird, or pigeon, so more clues are needed so he can make a final distinction.) "It waddles and swims in the water." You could also add sound if it is necessary. (3) "I am going someplace. See if you can guess where it is. I need my purse, and I will go in the car (or on the bus). When I get there, there will be cans of food, a bakery, some fruit, and milk. Can you guess where I'm going?" Try other places that are familiar to your child, such as the church, post office, gas station, library, park, or school.

Help your child name and identify unusual shapes (cone, pyramid, cube, hexagon) made out of wood, plastic, or paper. Use a replica of each shape before you expect the child to identify an outline or one-dimensional shape.

Help your child understand the relationship of familiar shapes to three-dimensional shapes (triangle/pyramid, circle/sphere, and square/cube).

Discuss and demonstrate opposites: big/little, large/small, more than/less than, hot/cold, and light/heavy.

Discuss a past or future activity so that your child can have experience in sequencing: "first we do this, then this, then this, and last we do this" (getting dressed, going someplace, returning home).

Activities in the Home and Community

Go to the local library or bookmobile. Help your child understand that we can learn about things from books.

Make a simple map for your child on a large piece of paper, a piece of unbleached muslin, a sheet, or an oil cloth and provide props (cars, people, houses) so your child can learn about the community.

Take your child places in the community where he can experience cultural differences (dress, language, customs).

Explore the community. Go where you can get free or low-cost materials: wood scraps from a lumber yard; paper ends from a newspaper office or publishing firm; styrofoam packing and material for building from a local department store; wallpaper and paint samples from a paint store; fabric pieces from factories or neighbors; magazines, toys, and dress-ups from second-hand stores or from friends; equipment, toys, and furniture from garage sales, auctions, or bazaars; posters or pictures from stores; or cardboard boxes from a furniture store.

Discuss a world globe in simple terms.

Go to interesting places of work and entertainment.

Provide your child with a box or drawer full of dress-up clothes and accessories. (Clothing of a school-age child often fits the preschooler better than does adult clothing.) Include jewelry, costumes, purses, hats, gloves, eyeglass frames with glass removed, flowers, and fans. Encourage dramatic play.

Save empty food cans, boxes, cartons, bags, and ribbons, and let your child play "store."

Point out to your child the different kinds of transportation vehicles and how they work.

Help your child make a bird feeder out of an empty milk carton, egg carton, metal jar ring, old doughnut, or paper plate. Assist in nest building: loosely weave yarn and string through the holes in a mesh bag and then hang the bag in a tree.

Help your child plant an inside garden. Select seeds that germinate rapidly (such as radishes or beans). Put dirt in an egg carton, muffin pan, empty milk or cottage cheese carton, or a glass container. Add seeds and slip the whole container into a plastic bag and twist it closed. Remove the bag when the seeds sprout, and place the container in a light place, but not in direct sunlight. Also plant bulbs and sprout seeds for eating or transplanting outdoors. Show your child the whole cycle of plants: seeds, plants, produce, seeds. You may want to use "peat-pots" in pots, baskets, barrels, bags, etc., for inside growing.

Help your child plant an outdoor garden. Select and prepare the soil. Obtain seeds from a store or from previous plants (you could use squash and melon seeds, avocado and fruit pits, or plant cuttings). Small seeds should be mixed with fine soil or sand; seed tapes, bulbs, and plants are also available. Help your child follow through by showing him how to water, weed, and protect plants from the elements. Help your child harvest the produce and eat it, or save the seeds for future plantings.

Sensory Perception

Because sensory perception is the first and most dependable method a young child has of gaining information about his world, special attention should be given to it. Many parents strongly object when a child tries to put everything into his mouth or when he tries to handle everything. Once the value of such behavior by a child is recognized, parents are able to cope with it and perhaps even encourage it when it is appropriate.

The child's five senses—sight, taste, smell, touch, and hearing—are vital to his learning. You may have noticed how your child looks at something as if he is really studying it, how most things go into his mouth (whether or not they are edible), or how he is always sniffing and smelling, wanting to touch and feel everything, and to hear sounds again and again or have them explained. From birth, the senses have been your child's most informative ways of learning about the world. Your child may not understand verbalization, but if the senses go to work, he can process information quite well for a child of limited experience.

For motor development, maturation is a key factor. But perceptual development is far more dependent on experiences and learning than on maturation. If the child doesn't have relevant experiences, he will lack the abilities needed for intellectual growth, for mastery of language

(Lugo and Hershey 1974), and for the development of later academic skills like paying attention, listening, and following instructions (Lillie 1975). The quality of perception affects such things as self-confidence, willingness to attack new tasks, relationships with others, and self-image.

Because the senses are so special and because each has a different function in learning, each one is discussed individually, together with some ideas for sharpening them. If you can think of ways to combine one or more of the senses in a single experience, it will be that much more meaningful.

Sight (Visual Perception)

By processing incoming visual stimuli, the child can make meaning or order out of his environment. But sometimes the child is fooled by what he sees because his thoughts and eyes are immature. The retina won't be completely developed until the child is about six years of age, and the child will be twelve or fourteen years old before his eyeball is adult size. These deficiencies, together with the shape of the eyeball, cause the child to be farsighted, so that only a small percentage of preschool children require glasses (Smart and Smart 1973). With age and experience, the child develops the ability to see things accurately and to organize these images in meaningful ways (Lugo and Hershey 1974). This ability is extremely important, because eighty percent of everything a child learns is learned through the sense of sight (Hendrick 1975).

A kindergarten teacher gave a drawing of the American flag to each five-year-old in her class and instructed each one to color it. Later in the day she was thumbing through the completed papers. She was disgusted, horrified, and angry when she came upon one which was not colored red, white, and blue. She called the child to her desk and reprimanded him thoroughly. The child felt ashamed and worthless. The teacher never bothered to check the child's perception of those colors; it was not until later that the teacher was told the child was red-green color blind! How anxious do you think this child was to color the next project?

Recognizing different forms (shapes) is important—it is the single most important visual skill needed for reading success. It isn't until the age of seven that a child no longer confuses the letter b with d and the letter p with g (Cratty 1970). The child needs to see whole words as well as individual letters, and this whole-part perception is used in activities other than reading. The younger the child, the more he pays attention to entire forms; but by the middle of the sixth year, he is able to relate parts to the whole (how a piece fits into a puzzle or how a wheel is part of a wagon, for example). The child will gather important information through seeing visual symbols, so it is important that he develops the whole-part perception necessary for learning basic sight words (Lugo and Hershey 1974) and for making other important visual discriminations like direction, shape, and location.

Activities for Sight Stimulation

Sort playing cards (first by color, then by suit, then by number).

Sort plastic chips or poker chips by color.

Sort objects by color, pattern, and size (large to small).

Match similar pictures or objects (increasing in difficulty or detail).

Match visual pattern or design of alphabet or other blocks.

Trace one of several overlapping designs.

Match dominoes by dots.

Sort colored paint chips. Use clear colors and only a few chips.

Match color chips by color, yarn to fabric, or lids to pans.

Paste parts of shapes over whole shapes (for instance, paste one-half and one-quarter of a circle on the whole circle).

Sort buttons (by color, size, or number of holes), seeds, or coins into egg carton cups.

Paste different sizes and colors of macaroni into a design.

Let your child talk about the characteristics of each of several shapes that you draw on the floor with tape or chalk (for instance, a star has five points, a triangle has three). Give your child some similar shapes, and let him place them inside the corresponding form.

Look around your environment and help your child identify things of similar shapes, colors, and other physical characteristics.

Help your child learn to match: a mother animal to her baby; parts to a whole, such as pieces to a puzzle or toy; or socks on laundry day.

Get individual body parts for a doll made of felt or paper. Ask your child what is needed for him to combine the parts to make a person.

Make simple left-to-right designs for your child to duplicate (blocks, finger in sand, paint, and yarn).

Take a simple picture and paste it onto cardboard. Let your child help design the lines for cutting it up to make a puzzle. Cut the puzzle and mix up the pieces; let your child put them back together. (Make it simple at first.)

Let your child help you repair broken objects (a toy, doll, plate, and so on).

Let your child sort things such as socks by size or by color.

Show your child how to use a prism, compass, thermometer, barometer, magnifying glass, magnet, and mirror.

Show your child how to use a camera and let him take some pictures.

Make and use fingerpaint—make a design and rub it out, use clear paint, and add colors. (See recipe section.)

Let your child measure and pour sand, flour, dry beans, rice, wood shavings, and water.

Make a paper circle out of one primary color (red, yellow, or blue). When your child has learned to recognize it, teach him another primary color and make a two-color wheel. Continue as he is ready.

Provide two to four patterns cut from a patterned paper or fabric (such as continuation of stripes or plaids or flowers). Let your child match another piece of the pattern to it.

Show your child how to take proper care of his eyes.

Take your child to a local optometrist. Have the optometrist show your child the equipment for checking eyes and making glasses.

Show your child a simple model of an eye.

Help your child explore depth perception (through water or from a height).

Show your child a group of pictures with one differing from the others; help your child to locate the one that is different.

Games

Play picture bingo. Use cards with an animal's picture in each of nine squares. Draw picture cards from a pile and place them on the matching square. The first one to cover three spaces in a row wins the game.

Play card games such as lotto and "Old Maid."

Go "fishing." Make a pole out of a stick, a string, and a paper clip. Make a variety of pictures illustrating a pair of opposite concepts (such as float-sink, rough-smooth, same-different, hard-soft, work-play, large-small, boy-girl, happy-sad, and so on). Attach a small magnet to each picture. Let your child "fish" for the pictures over a barrier and then place the pictures in appropriate piles. (Use only one set of opposites at a time.)

Language

Use a story book and say, "I see a _____. Can you find it?"

Help your child identify opposites from pictures (a child running and a child sleeping, a bird flying and a bird sitting in a tree).

Listen to your child describe things he likes most to look at or see.

Help your child identify traffic signs by color, shape, or wording.

Help your child put experiences into words (a trip to the zoo, a party).

Help your child watch for important signs in the community (hospital, school).

Help your child describe the different seasonal changes.

Visualization

See if your child can find some objects hidden in simple pictures (or certain shapes in a puzzle).

Help your child discover reversals (a boy facing left, a boy facing right).

Encourage your child to reproduce parquetry designs.

Let your child stack things such as blocks, cartons, cans, paper plates, paper cups, measuring cups and spoons, pots, shoes, socks, jars, or hats by color, shape, or size.

Provide your child with inlaid puzzles made of wood, paper, or cardboard; let him put the puzzles together.

Place pictures of animals, fruit, or some other group of objects around the room.

Give your child corresponding pictures and see if he can match them.

Hide several objects. Show your child a similar one, and ask him to find the hidden object in the room.

Let your child look at you closely. Then change something about your appearance and let him guess what it was (put on your glasses or a hat, remove your coat, and so on).

Place some directional signs (such as arrows, footprints, and so on) around the room and let your child follow them.

Show your child how shadows are made. A flashlight may be helpful.

Place several small objects on a table. Cut "shadows," outlines of the shapes of the objects, out of black construction paper. Let your child place each object with its shadow.

From pictures, cards, or objects, show your child how to identify things that go together (baby and bottle, knife and fork, hen and chick, horse and colt).

When a child shows interest, watch for and identify shapes in clouds, trees, mountains, shadows, and so on.

Draw a shape on a piece of paper and let your child paste yarn over the shape.

Taste Perception

How young children love the taste of some things—and hate the taste of others! Although adults have taste buds only on the surface of the tongue, children of preschool age have them generously distributed on the insides of their cheeks, in their throats, and on their tongues, too, making them highly sensitive to taste (Smart and Smart 1973). Sensitivity to tastes varies with each child, just like any other aspect of human growth varies. Some preschoolers can taste bitter foods, for instance, while some cannot taste them at all; there is variation of sensitivity to the other three tastes (salty, sweet, and sour). Breakfast is generally the meal that is most enjoyed by young children (Smart and Smart 1973); meat is a highly preferred food for all meals.

Eating stimulates not only the child's sense of taste, but also his sensations of smell, sight, and touch (with his fingers *and* his mouth), even though he may not know it. A teacher of four-year-olds was pre-assessing the knowledge of the children regarding the relationship of taste to smell. She asked, "Do our noses help us taste things?" The reply was a unanimous "No!" Expecting the opposite answer, she asked, "Why not?" The children replied, "Because our noses don't have teeth!"

Sometimes the child forgets the task of eating because he is so excited about savoring the aroma, looking at the colors and the variety of the food, or exploring the textures. Don't get too upset if your child exercises these senses with nonedible things. Often he can't tell whether they are nonedible without exploring them with his senses. (More information about developing good eating habits may be found in the *Food and Nutrition* section of Chapter One.)

Activities for Stimulation of the Sense of Taste

Provide new foods occasionally and encourage your child to taste them.

Discuss the different tastes of the same food: a potato can be mashed, baked, french fried, pan fried, or eaten raw; a carrot can be juiced, cooked, or eaten raw.

Discuss the general use of food (cereal for breakfast, vegetables for dinner, or whatever is common to your family).

Discuss what your child likes to taste best.

Show your child how to take good care of his mouth and teeth.

Take your child to the dentist for a checkup. Have the dentist show your child a model of teeth and the correct brushing procedure.

Have your child hold his nose and try to identify familiar foods by taste only.

Show your child a model or picture of the tongue and where the various taste buds are located.

Let your child taste some things that are raw and then cooked, and compare them. Preschoolers often prefer raw to cooked vegetables.

Provide foods with a variety of textures (soft, hard, chewy, liquid) for your child to taste. Chewing some foods may give your child a sense of power.

Blindfold your child and let him identify familiar tastes.

Show your child foods that look alike (powdered sugar and soda, salt and granulated sugar). Let him taste them to identify them.

See other activities listed in the *Food and Nutrition* section of Chapter One.

Smell (Olfactory Perception)

Little is known about the sense of smell except that the newborn turns away from noxious odors and the adult can distinguish over four thousand odors (Lugo and Hershey 1974). In between these two age extremes, the child knows that some smells are pleasant and that some are offensive. Occasionally he hesitates to smell something because of the fear that it will be strong or unpleasant. Try to help your child develop his sense of smell, because it can help him make good decisions.

Activities for Stimulation of the Sense of Smell

Put foods with different odors in different jars. Have corresponding pictures of the foods, and let your child match the pictures to the jars.

Have your child close his eyes and identify various familiar things by smell only.

Let your child tell you about his favorite smells.

Explain to your child what certain smells indicate: mother baking, freshly mowed lawn, bacon for breakfast, freshly polished shoes, smoke from a fire.

Add a fragrance (such as peppermint, lemon, or perfume) to your child's paste, paint, or clay.

Introduce your child to some strong fragrances such as onion, soap, cinnamon, cloves, cantaloupe, mint, rose petals, orange peel, lemonade, leather, peppermint, eucalyptus, anise (licorice), shoe polish, or perfume.

Teach your child the proper care of his nose (blowing, cleaning, caring for nosebleed).
Show your child how a cold affects the ability to taste.
Show your child a replica of a nose.

Touch (Tactile Perception)

When you go to grocery, fabric, variety, and other kinds of stores, don't you like to pick up and examine the toilet paper, the velvet, or the plants? Your child wants to touch things, too, but sometimes you tell him *NO,* and then you go ahead and touch the same things. This is difficult for your child to understand: why is it all right for adults to touch, but not for children? If you have objects around the house that the child is not supposed to handle (such as fragile ceramics, antiques, or similar treasures), why don't you show him which ones they are, and then tell him why he shouldn't touch them? Be sure to show him the things he *can* play with.

One type of touching doesn't get much attention—the feeling of being touched or of touching someone else. When a tender hand is placed in yours, you feel that everything is all right and that someone really cares about you. For a young child, sitting close to another person or on his parent's lap makes reading and talking special. (As your child grows bigger and older, he probably won't sit on your lap or hold your hand any more; then you will probably miss the closeness of these preschool years.) When you cross a street or go for a walk with your preschooler and request that he hold your hand, sometimes the child may resent this because he wants to feel independent.

Feeling can be *unpleasant,* too. When your child scrapes a knee or pinches a finger, your attention and reassurance are appreciated. Don't "baby" the child, but let him know that it is all right to cry occasionally, that you have empathy, and that you will help to reduce the pain.

Don't forget that many parts of the body, not just fingers and feet, feel. Friendly scuffles on the floor or in the grass are often invigorating.

Activities for Stimulation of the Sense of Touch

Encourage your child to walk barefoot on different surfaces: cement, carpet, wet grass, wet and dry sand, wood floor, gravel, and water.
Blindfold your child and hand him some objects that are similar except for one dimension; then ask your child to hand back the "biggest," "roughest," and so on.
Help your child make a collage of various textures.
Help your child make papier-mâché out of shredded paper and liquid starch, then help him form it into any object. Let the object dry, and then paint it.
Have your child close his eyes and try to make a design in a pegboard with pegs.
Make some cards covered with textured fabrics on one side. Play "Old Maid" for textures (sandpaper, velvet, or plastic) or "texture lotto." Then play the same game blindfolded.

Use "texture lotto" cards to talk about opposites (such as slick-rough).

Go for a walk with your child and gather natural things to make a collage (picture) out of upon returning.

Gather the ingredients and then help your child make fingerpaint. (See recipes section.) Then add different textures to it, such as sand or glitter, or add colors (not more than two). Encourage your child to use his fingertips as well as his whole hand in painting; sometimes he could even *feet* paint!

Give your child a pile of different-textured fabrics and let him stack them into "like" piles: soft, rough, smooth, scratchy.

Help your child cut pictures out of magazines that show different emotions. Discuss the emotions and then place them into appropriate piles—sad, happy, and so on. Explain that emotions are another way of "feeling."

Show your child the proper care of the skin—cleaning, lubricating (with lotion or cream), and protecting from weather and harm.

Let your child feel familiar things; then ask him to put them into a sack and put gloves on his hands. The child then feels the things with gloved hands and tries to identify them.

Put familiar things inside a sock. Let your child feel and identify them.

Instead of blindfolding the child or asking your child to close his eyes, provide a cute mask (without holes for eyes) for your child to wear during many of these activities.

Language

Talk about the proper way to handle things (such as small pets, fragile things, hot things, and babies).

Define terms and give your child corresponding touch experiences: sticky, gooey, lumpy, sharp, cold, brittle, and elastic.

Let your child tell about his favorite things to touch.

Help your child identify the parts of his hand (palm, wrist, joints, thumb, and fingers).

Hearing (Auditory Perception)

Strange as it may seem, the ability to discriminate *sounds* is more important in beginning to read than is *visual* discrimination. The child's abilities to make sound discriminations, to select relevant sounds and to disregard others, to associate sounds with their sources, to perceive rhythm and variation in patterns, to develop memory so he can remember and repeat sound patterns, and to solve problems through language sound combinations are all part of good listening (Brophy 1975).

At birth, hearing is one of the least developed senses because amniotic fluid stops up the middle ear so that sound waves cannot penetrate to the inner ear, and sense cells in the inner ear are only partially developed. Within the first few days of life, however, a child can tell the location of sound (Hurlock 1972).

You may often wonder if your preschooler has any hearing at all. He may ignore your request to say or do something, "shutting you out" for several reasons: he may be too involved in a project, he doesn't like to be nagged, he wants to give you the same treatment you dish out, he is taking time to think through a response, or he is unresponsive for many other reasons. If you suspect your child really could have a hearing problem, and is not shutting you out for any of the above reasons, seek professional help. Remember, too, that hearing can be injured by loud noises, so you may need to help your child adjust the sounds he listens to on radio, television, transportation vehicles, or at sports events.

Hearing unidentified sounds (sudden, loud, unfamiliar, or continual noise) may cause the child to become fearful. Help your child relieve these fears by showing him the source of the noise whenever possible.

Activities for Stimulation of the Sense of Sound
Interaction Activities

Have your child close his eyes. Move to different parts of the room and say something (or use a bell or whistle). Have your child point to where the sound is coming from.

Have your child close his eyes. Give him instructions ("Go to the door") and then continual directions ("Straight ahead, to the side") until he reaches a destination with his eyes still closed.

Prerecord sounds that occur in various rooms of the house. Play them back and ask your child to identify the sound and where it occurs (water in the kitchen or bathroom, mixer in the kitchen, shaver in the bathroom, clock in the bedroom).

Make sound tubes: fill two containers with different items (two rice, two beans, two rocks, two sand, two water). Let your child shake one set and then try to match it to the other set.

Take a walk with your child; stop and listen to sounds often.

Have your child close his eyes. Speak to him in different emotional tones. See if he can guess if you're happy, sad, or mad.

Ask your child to imitate sounds—sounds from around the house or sounds of transportation, animals, toys, or weather.

Give your child from one to three directions. See if he can follow them. ("Stand up, turn around, take a cookie.")

Teach your child some simple songs and finger games.

Say a word and have your child try to think of its opposite. Keep it simple—*hot, quiet, slow, up*.

Let your child show his interpretation of various kinds of music through simple dance or movement.

Go on a visit to a music studio—listen to a band, orchestra, group, or soloist.

Make up a story using sounds and let your child identify them. "Then we heard a . . . (make sound like a train) and we knew we were at . . . (the depot)." Let your child add sounds and ideas to the story.

Help your child identify parts of the body with articles of clothing. "Your arm goes in the . . . (sleeve). Your shirt goes over your . . . (head)."

Do rhyming activities: "Put your finger on your nose and then your toes." "Put your finger on your chest, take a rest." "Stand up tall, be a ball."

Ask your child to point to various parts of a doll's body and then to corresponding parts of his own body.

Discuss prepositions and let your child practice them with his body and with objects. "Go under the table." "Ride around the box." "Put the toy on the shelf."

Help your child care for his personal needs through encouragement and instruction (how to wash, brush teeth, bathe, use toilet, comb hair, and dress).

Take your child with you when you go shopping and run errands. Explain where you are going, why, and who you'll see: "Today we are going to the gas station where we (or the attendant) will put gas in the car so it will go. Then we will go to the bakery to get bread," or "Today we will go to the market to get vegetables that are grown by the farmer." Make it simple and informative rather than a complicated, running lecture.

Give your child experience in making appropriate choices based on developmental abilities ("Do you want to wear your red shirt or your blue one today?" "Shall we make cookies or a cake?" "Do you want to hear a story or play a short game before bedtime?").

Discuss cause and effect events with your child: "If _____ (we water the plants), then _____ (they will grow)."

Help your child recall facts from memory: "In the winter, _____." "In the summer, the grass is _____." "At the park you _____."

Show your child some pictures and then make a sound that goes with one of them. Let your child select the corresponding picture.

Give experiences in discriminating sounds (begin with only two dimensions at first—loud and soft, fast and slow; later add one more or a combination): bells, household sounds, animal sounds, and so on.

Combine sounds with physical activities: stamp to loud music, tiptoe to soft, jump to slow, skip to fast.

Compare sounds: small bell and cow bell, car horn and toy horn, metal hammer and rubber hammer, metal pan and metal cup.

Duplicate various rhythms by clapping, playing a rhythm instrument, or striking an object (dowels, metal containers).

Place objects that make sound (whistle, bell, finger cymbals, shakers, harmonica, rhythm sticks, horn) in a box. Let your child demonstrate how to play each one, sometimes using the instrument and sometimes pantomiming.

Let your child dramatize a favorite story and make sounds or actions of the characters (for example, if the story is about a farm, let your child make sounds or actions as each animal is mentioned) or point to an object (animal, train, bird, fire engine) in a picture and let your child make an appropriate corresponding sound.

Have a tape with recorded sounds and pictures that correspond to the sounds. As the tape is played, let your child select the picture to match it.

Give your child experiences with vibration—rubber band, stringed instrument, tuning fork, larynx, ruler on the corner of a table.

Show your child how to use the phone (dialing, answering, calling, being courteous).

Obtain a stethoscope from a clinic, doctor's office, school, or library and let your child listen to his heart.

Teach your child the proper care of his ears.

Acquaint your child with a person who wears a hearing aid.

Show your child a model of the ear and explain how people hear.

Play instruction games like "Simon Says," "Hokey Pokey," or "Do as I'm Doing."

Language

Discuss music terms: high, low, loud, soft, fast, slow. Have your child turn his back while you demonstrate the various terms, and let your child identify them.

Discuss what certain sounds mean: siren, chimes, whistle, church bell, thunder.

Let your child tell a story—it can be either original or repeated.

Let your child make and identify transportation sounds (train, airplane, boat, motorcycle, horse).

Talk about comparisons (his body to yours or to a baby's, a tricycle to a car, a dog to a horse).

Explain the characteristics of different instruments, such as woodwind, percussion, or string. Give your child some replicas and let him put them into the correct groups: blow (woodwind), strike (percussion), pluck (string), shake (bells).

Encourage your child to be independent. Say, "You can do it." "Try . . ." "The label in your shirt goes in the back." "Loosen the laces first." "Sit on the floor and then put this foot in this shoe."

Talk with your child about family members, their characteristics, and their responsibilities. Start with the immediate family and then go on to other familiar relatives.

When your child does something wrong or unacceptable, gently explain the situation and kindly help to remedy the error; don't embarrass him in front of others.

When your child expresses fear, help him work through it gradually: "I know you feel afraid when your room is dark. I'll leave the hall light on." "That is a big dog. We can look at him from here."

Explain responsibility and praise your child's attempts to fulfill tasks: "You did a good job . . . (taking out the garbage, setting the table, bringing in the mail, putting your toys away)."

When your child is involved in a project, give a few minutes' warning so that he will have time to finish; don't expect immediate termination for your convenience.

Explain limits. Use positive statements by telling your child what he *can* do rather than what he *can't* do. Give simple reasons.

Use two things that sound alike (goat-boat, Faun-John). Talk about similarities ("You can ride a goat or a boat") and differences ("One goes in the water; the other goes on land"). Other similarities and differences should be explained (how children may have the same hair and eye coloring, but be different in height or weight, for example).

Place a set of cards out on the table (the number of pairs depends on your child's maturity—few at first, more later). Ask your child to select and name two pictures that rhyme (fish-dish, cat-bat, jar-car, coat-boat, house-mouse).

Ask riddles involving letter sounds. "There is someone you know whose name begins like train and who plays with you in the sandpile. Can you guess who it is?" (Tracy) "I know an animal that lives in the woods, has a bushy tail, and whose name sounds like box. Can you guess what it is?" (Fox) "I know something that has three wheels, you can ride on it, and it sounds like Mike. Can you guess what it is?" (Trike) Let your child make up some riddles, too.

Show your child different objects (wheel, shoe, block, string, box, cookie, toy) and ask your child to help think of different things that could be done with them.

Help your child learn about sound; use a yardstick or cans and a string to show how sound travels.

Show or tell how various people protect their ears from weather and sound.

Listening

Make sounds behind a screen and let your child try to identify them.
Record voices or sounds on a tape recorder; let your child listen.

Play prerecorded sounds. Let your child identify them or follow the instructions.

Listen quietly and then see if your child can identify some of the sounds in the environment.

Help your child identify different machines by sound—egg beater, razor, mixer, vacuum cleaner, sewing machine, and building tools and vehicles (such as a saw, cement truck, grader, or bulldozer).

Expose your child to different kinds of music—classical, symphonic, rock, popular, marches, folk songs, jazz. Tell him the names of the selections.

Describe a procedure and let your child do it (dressing, making something, getting something, going someplace).

Say nursery rhymes and see if your child can select rhyming words (Bo Peep-sheep, quick-stick, horn-corn). Explain to your child that the word *rhyme* means words that sound alike.

Read simple, appropriate poetry to your child. Help him make up his own poems.

Tell a story using sounds to represent the characters (stomping for the elephant, whistling for the bird, humming for a child, clapping for thunder). Encourage your child to participate.

Help your child learn to screen out the unimportant sounds and listen to the important ones in a noisy situation.

Divergent Thinking

Divergent thinking refers to the ability to think of something other than what is most commonly thought of in a given situation. It is most helpful in problem solving because it stimulates different solutions or ideas rather than only one *right* way to react or perform. You could even call it creative thinking.

Your Child's Need for Creativity

Perhaps up to now it has been easier to tell your child what to do and then to have him simply follow through. But those days are numbered. With developing independence and autonomy, he wants to make more of his own decisions. Your child wants to learn how to solve problems by reasoning them through. Although he will make many mistakes and misjudgments because of his inability to explain or logically resolve problems, early reasoning is part of cognitive development.

Unfortunately our society stresses convergent thinking—selecting one precise, correct answer—but usually a problem has a number of good solutions. Rather than applying one solution and letting it go at that, we are now encouraged to think creatively and to generate new information emphasizing variety and quantity. "Is there *another* way that it could be done?" "What *else* could you do?" "Is there a *better* way?" "How would *you* do it?" "Let's see what happens when we try *this*." "Have you *thought* about that?"

The ability to think divergently develops slowly. If you value your child's ideas and respond positively to them, he will feel secure enough to resolve problems rather than to always try to figure out what *you* want him to do. Without demanding performance or making your child feel interrogated, ask thought-provoking (but not too many) questions like "what?" "how?" and "why?" when opportunities arise ("What do you think Daddy would like for his birthday?"). Give your child time to think of an answer. You should also help your child answer his own questions: "Let's see if we can find out," or "Maybe this will help us." Even unsuccessful solutions can be a good learning experience, but try to give guidance so your child won't get into too many discouraging situations: "That was a good try. The wagon is still stuck, so maybe you could _____ (empty it out, get a board for the wheel to go up on, and so on)." Let your preschooler try things on his own (with you standing by in case a hint or demonstration is needed).

Using Language to Stimulate Creativity

Language and thinking are so closely linked that they are almost inseparable. At times you may be tempted to lecture or to explain things that are difficult for you to put into words. They are also difficult for your child to understand. Whenever possible, involve your preschooler with actual and real objects (rather than pictures or replicas) so that he can manipulate and get the feel of them. Then discuss them. That's one of the easiest ways to learn.

You can have some fun discussions together. Suppose that instead of reading your child a story you read part of it and then say, "What do you think will happen? If you were the child, what would you do?" Use pictures to stimulate talking times. At other times, brainstorm and see how many answers the two of you can produce for a given situation. Discuss ways to rearrange your child's room together. Decorate for a party. Talk about fun trips. Role play, switching roles, so that your child pretends to be you and you imitate your child. Provide props for dramatic play, or let your child tell an occasional story or experience to you or the family using cutouts and a flannelboard. You might be surprised by what he thinks is important.

When your child answers a question, your inclination may be to say, "No, that's not right." But it's better for you to withhold that comment and substitute, "Why do you think that?" "Tell me more," or a similar inquiry. You may find out that the answer *does* have merit. If your child is confused, you can clarify—but only if you know how he is thinking. The answer may relate to a perfectly true concept or happening, but if you don't understand your child's thoughts, you may think he is wrong. If you always act this way, soon your child will quit offering ideas.

Using Objects to Stimulate Creativity

Let's look at examples of divergent thinking. Suppose you give your child a stack of plastic chips in three colors (red, yellow, and blue), three sizes (small, medium, and large), and three shapes (circle, square, and triangle). Then ask him to put those that are alike in three piles. The child will probably sort them all by color, or all by size, or all by shape. He can only take one attribute (color, or size, or shape) into account at once. After sorting them into piles according to one attribute (probably color), he may have difficulty figuring out another method (size or shape) of sorting.

Conceptual abilities involve grouping (putting similar things together), ordering (arranging objects in increasing or decreasing size or in sequences), perceiving common relationships between items (telling how they are alike), understanding cause and effect (knowing what will happen if you do or don't do something), matching identical items, and conserving (realizing that form may change appearance when quantity remains unchanged). Since most of these abilities are hard for the preschool child, please have patience. He will improve with age and experience.

You may not have realized that art experiences are good exercises for the brain, eye, and hand. Deciding *what* to do and *how* to do it sharpens the child's intellect; a good way is by making a collage. Discovering how to use materials and tools stimulates inventiveness, flexibility, and creativity. Too often children are expected to do only what they are told, and then only when and how they are told to do it. This really limits motivation and opportunities. Instead, parents should stimulate and challenge their child's capabilities. Children are more interested in processes and in manipulating materials than they are in a finished product (although older children typically decide upon and complete a project).

Remember the preschooler's inexperience with language and environment and his desire to do things beyond his skills. Because the child may grow impatient or be easily discouraged, don't overemphasize mechanical learning (such as strict instructions, conformity, excellence, pressure).

Help your child put his feelings into appropriate language and arrange his environment for learning, and provide activities and materials to help him develop skills. Above all, love your child during these frustrating years. If you do all these things, there is a good chance he will become a creative, divergent thinker. What a contribution your child could make—you may have a budding scientist, artist, researcher, teacher, or diplomat!

Activities to Stimulate Divergent Thinking

Many times in the course of a preschooler's day problems arise—but they are "teachable moments" when you can help your child reason and find solutions. When your child can't get a shoe on or can't make a toy work or when a friend takes a toy away, help him reason through the problems as well as the solutions. There should be several ways to resolve the problems. Say, "Let's see what's wrong here." "How could we fix that?" "Is there something else we could do?" "What do you think we should do?" *Never* make your child feel interrogated or inferior; value his suggestions and at least give them a try before rejecting them.

Activities to Do Together

Show parts of an object (wheel, handle, bed) and see if your child can identify the object as the parts are put together (such as a wagon). This helps him see part-whole relationships.

Assemble homemade or commercial puzzles.

Give experiences to your child to move his body in space; this makes your child aware of his body and what it can do. Use prepositions to indicate desired position and give directions to follow, but leave room for creativity on the part of your child.

Let your child guess which of two objects would be heaviest (weigh more) and then find out by using a scale or by letting him hold things in his hand.

Help your child experience speed, such as by walking slowly and then running fast.

Help your child take some simple toys or objects apart, identify the parts, and then put them back together.

Make a "feel" bag by putting several items into a paper or cloth bag. Let your child identify the objects by feeling them through the bag's opening.

Make a "guess" box. Put a familiar object inside a box and give some simple clues about what it is. See if your child can guess what it is, and then show him the object.

Place several objects on a table. Let your child examine them, and then cover them up. Remove one while the child isn't looking, and see if he can remember what it was.

Demonstrate for your child how to use a siphon to empty a fish tank, tub, or bucket.

Let your child play in and explore water—wash, make food (from a concentrate) and creative materials (dry paint), drink, float or sink objects, or watch water evaporate. Also introduce the other two forms of water: ice and steam.

Let your child show and tell you different things he can do with his different body parts.

Let your child use some self-correcting materials (such as puzzles or graded holes and pegs) so that he can tell if they're done correctly.

Let your child use building blocks.

Activities for Sequencing

Give your child a series of three or four pictures to arrange in a proper sequence (whole apple, bites out of apple, core).

Give your child a series of objects to arrange in order (large to small, light to dark).

Let your child arrange a series of pictures according to time sequence.

Make a design with three to five beads (or objects) beginning at your child's left and going to his right. Ask him to duplicate the design.

Language Activities

Ask your child questions about familiar happenings: (1) John wants a new toy that Susan has. What should he do? (2) Mother is going to the store. What should she buy? (3) It will soon be Peter's birthday. What do you think he'd like? (4) When it gets to be bedtime, what do you need to do? (5) What shall we take to eat on our picnic? (6) What kind of clothes should we wear in the winter? In the rain? In the summer? (7) How many different ways can we ride to grandmother's?

When you ask a question and your child responds with reasoning that seems uncommon or unexpected, say, "Why do you think so?" or "Tell me more about that." There may be a rational reason for his response.

Help your child learn to count to ten—not just by memory, but with meaning. ("Three people, three napkins. One for you, one for you, one for you. That makes three.")

Help your child understand the meanings of *first, second,* and *last.*

On a tape or behind a screen, make different sounds and see if your child can identify them by listening to the tape or without looking behind the screen.

Give your child two pictures to use to make up a story. As he becomes better at making up stories, add another picture or two.

Stimulate *wh* skills by asking simple questions (where? what? when? and why?).

Classification Activities

Show your child a few items that are related somehow (in color, use, or composition) and help your child identify the similarities and differences. (Differences are easiest to discern.)

Obtain two sets of matching pictures (such as those on "Old Maid" cards or lotto games) and let your child put them in pairs.

Have a variety of pictures and ask your child to sort things that go together (four- and two-legged animals; things that fly or swim; farm and zoo animals; two- and four-wheeled vehicles).

When your child shows readiness and understanding, give him experience with opposites (loud-soft, day-night, hot-cold, wet-dry, rough-smooth, and hard-soft).

Introduce the concept of *middle* after your child learns about big and little.

Provide experiences with comparisons (objects, structures, animals, shoes).

Language Development and Use

A group of children under eight years old were discussing the events of the new year and making resolutions. One child asked, "What is a resolution?" Another one quickly volunteered, "That's when there is a war."

Kimberly, age three, was bothered by the fact that her mother had made tapioca pudding for lunch and was trying to gain sympathy for having had to eat it. She asked, "Grandma, do you like tapioca?" "Yes," was her grandmother's answer. Silently Kimberly thought over the situation and then said, "Well, I don't like tapioca because it has so many lumpies in it."

It was the fall of the year and baseball was in the air. Tim, a four-year-old, followed the World Series games with his father. Excitedly he tried to inform a friend, "Today the Dodgers won, and tomorrow they won, and now if they only win yesterday, they will be the whole *winners!"*

The above examples indicate the inaccuracy or inefficiency of language used by young children. Just because they *use* certain words or terms doesn't mean they *understand* what they are saying.

Various Language Aspects

Basically, language is the ability to talk to others and to have them understand what has been said. Sometimes your children don't do as you say, and sometimes you have a hard time getting across the messages you intend, but you have to admit that being able to communicate is exciting—although sometimes confusing.

There is more to language than just words. Listening, following directions, hearing sounds accurately, attaching meanings to words and sentences, and learning other *receptive* skills are also vital. The child needs to be able to express his thoughts in an understandable way, to increase the number and quality of his words, to use words freely and easily, to put words into sequences that express complex thoughts, to use proper sentence structures, and to use other *expressive* skills. In other words, listening (*receptive*) and speaking (*expressive*) abilities need to be effectively combined (Lillie 1975).

Language Skills at Various Ages

It may be surprising to learn that most language skills are acquired by the age of four or five at the latest (McCarthy 1954; Menyuk 1963). Language development is complex, but some researchers think that children gain skills from imitation and from reinforcement (encouragement from others).

The child's use of sentences improves as he becomes older. He uses one-word sentences by eighteen months, two- or three-word sentences by thirty months, complete sentences averaging about four words by forty months, and average five-word sentences by seventy-eight months (McCarthy 1954). Sentence type proceeds from active (a noun or a verb) to negative, followed by questioning and then by passive (Smart and Smart 1973). Remember how your child's first words were "Go!" "Ball!" "Cookie!" "Come!" or something similar? Then at the age of two his favorite words were "No" and "Don't." Then came those endless questions—"Why?" and "What?" It was a relief when he moved on

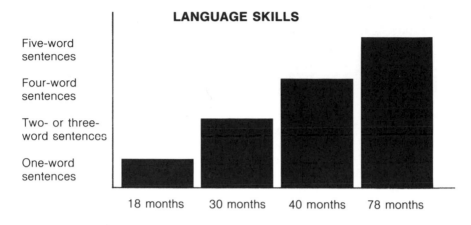

LANGUAGE SKILLS

Five-word sentences

Four-word sentences

Two- or three-word sentences

One-word sentences

| 18 months | 30 months | 40 months | 78 months |

Reference: Smart and Smart, 1973

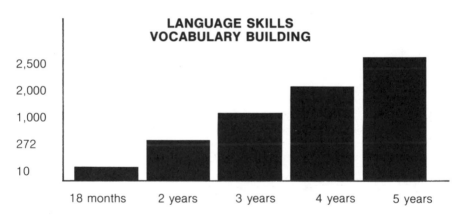

LANGUAGE SKILLS
VOCABULARY BUILDING

2,500

2,000

1,000

272

10

| 18 months | 2 years | 3 years | 4 years | 5 years |

(Even though most of the language skills are acquired by the ages of four or five, the vocabulary rapidly increases. Children gain skills for learning new words, learning a new definition, and learning new uses for old words.)

Reference: Hurlock, 1972

to his present stage: enjoying conversations and still keeping some of his former patterns (negative responses and questions).

The order of the child's understanding is different: active first ("Let's go bye-bye" and "Give me the doggie"), then questioning ("Where's the ball?" "Where's your nose?"), followed by passive ("My ball is gone") and negative ("Don't touch the vase") (Smart and Smart 1973).

Although *most* language skills are acquired by the age of four or five, vocabulary is not finalized by then; it increases by acquiring new words and by learning new definitions and learning uses for old words. Vocabulary increases quickly, as is shown by these averages and ages: the average person knows ten words at eighteen months, twenty words at twenty-four months, two hundred and seventy-two words at two years (Hurlock 1972), about one thousand words at three years, about two thousand words at four years, and about twenty-five hundred words at five years. Children today have larger vocabularies and more complex sentence structures than children did a generation ago, perhaps due to more time spent watching television and talking to adults and due to increased emphasis on preschool education (Lugo and Hershey 1974). Of course, there are wide individual differences among children, and it's hard to count the words they use at different ages, but the second year is a period of especially rapid development. Thought speeds up and becomes more precise and flexible. Verbal symbols make problem solving much easier. Having the vocabulary that enables a child to call a thing by its name helps, too. If you listen carefully, you will often hear your child talking to himself during various activities, always from his point of view. As socialization develops, your child learns the expectations of his culture, more complex sentence structures (by five he is using all eight parts of speech), more vocabulary and longer sentences, and new sound combinations. Now he can also replace physical behaviors with verbal ones (he doesn't hit and grab as much, and instead he uses more suggestions and requests).

There are some simple guidelines for language activity at various ages. A child of two and a half can sing or say short rhymes (nursery rhymes or commercials) and can react to sound, and he wants someone to enjoy it with him. At three he can understand and use simple verbs, pronouns, prepositions, and adjectives, and he can use complete sentences some of the time. At four a child can connect events and recent experiences and can carry out two simple directions in sequence ("get your shoe and bring it to mother"). A five-year-old may mispronounce some sounds, but he speaks intelligibly, converses with others casually, uses pronouns correctly, and uses the grammar of those adults who are around him (Masland 1969).

What You Can Do to Stimulate Language Skills

You have a strong influence on your child's thinking and language development. You can help by listening attentively, by providing stimulating topics for conversation (an animal, an object, a trip), by encouraging conversation, by asking questions that require more than a one-word (yes or no) answer, by helping him to listen accurately, and by finding out about programs for preschool language development (Hendrick 1975).

Sometimes telling what you want is more helpful than showing what you want (generally for three-year-olds), and it is sometimes hard for the young child to learn through observation alone. If you gain his attention, label objects and actions, and then add explanations, understanding is easier for the child (Brophy 1975). It is helpful, too, if there are visual aids to accompany your discussions when possible (such as a picture of a horse when you are discussing horses), because it is hard for your child to think about things that are not present.

We think talking is so simple and common, but it's actually quite complicated. Talking requires coordination of the lips, tongue, teeth, palate, jaws, cheeks, voice, and breath (Holt 1967), so you should be understanding of your child's mispronunciations and inability to make certain sound combinations; let him work them out at his own speed. Your child can understand *much* more than he can verbalize.

Another part of language also needs consideration: the nonverbal messages you send and receive (*body language*). Your child is a great follower; you are the leader. If you tell him one thing with your voice ("Hurry up!") and another thing with your body (just sitting there calmly), chances are very high that your child will follow your actions. If you tell him to get ready for supper while you sit and read the paper, you really have no right to get mad when he continues playing. Your child will pick up your attitude—no matter how well hidden you think it is. He needs all the help you can give in forming a positive, pleasant attitude. The world is sometimes difficult for a preschooler; he wants to see the world as a wonderful place and be accepted and liked by friendly people. You are his model; your child is your mirror.

Activities to Encourage Language Development

It appears somewhat superficial to devote a single section to language activities when they are vital to each and every topic in this book. However, the importance of good opportunities for listening and speaking cannot be overemphasized. When one can understand and communicate well, he develops a good self-image and can make a contribution to himself and to society.

Activities to Encourage Awareness of Verbal and Nonverbal Language

Make facial expressions and let your child identify and reproduce them while looking in a mirror.

Show your child pictures of familiar objects with inconsistencies and let your child find them (a dog with an elephant's trunk, a cat eating with a knife and fork).

Show your child pictures and let him discuss them with you (actions of characters or seasons of the year, for instance).

Show your child pictures of things that have essential parts missing

68

DEVELOPMENT OF LANGUAGE ACTIVITY

Age	Skills
2½	Can sing or say short rhymes and can react to sound. Wants someone to enjoy it with him.
3	Understands and uses simple verbs, pronounces prepositions and adjectives and some complete sentences.
4	Connects events and recent experiences. Can carry out two simple directions in sequence.
5	Speaks intelligibly but may mispronounce some sounds. Converses with others casually, uses pronouns correctly, and uses grammar of those adults who are around him.

Reference: Maslund, 1969

(such as one eye on a face or a dog with no head). Let him identify the missing part.

Present pictures showing motion (such as running or washing); let your child describe and demonstrate the motion.

Show your child a variety of pictures. Then help him identify something that they all have in common (for instance, things we do in the summer or things that fly). When your child has mastered this activity, present two general pictures (like the sun and moon) and let him separate pictures into appropriate categories (things we do during the day, things we do during the night).

Put several objects on a table and let your child examine them. Cover them and then remove one. Let him guess what is missing.

Provide experiences involving your child with another person (housekeeping, sandbox, teeter-totter) and calling for conversation and cooperation.

Let your child help cook.

Let your child help care for another member of the family (baby or grandparent).

Let your child arrange sequence cards, and then discuss why he thinks some things happen before others.

Tell a story or play a game with each of you using a puppet.

Have family night and let each family member take part.

Show your child a familiar color. Let him name it, and then point to objects in the room that are the same color.

Teach your child some fun songs, and sing them often.

Do finger games and fingerplays.

Help your child imitate various rhythms by clapping, using music, or pretending to move like various animals.

Give your child some simple directions or descriptions on how to move, using large or small muscles.

Encourage development of your child's tongue muscles by blowing, sucking, laughing, and humming.

Take a walk around the neighborhood and let your child talk about what he sees.

Make finger, sack, hand, string, or stick puppets using salt boxes, paper cups, oatmeal boxes, paper sacks, fabrics, potatoes, or miscellaneous items.

Make a puppet stage out of a box and fabric and have a puppet show.

Games

Play rhyming games: "I saw a cat and he had a _____ (rat, hat, bat)."

Play the *preposition game.* Tell your child some ways to use his body ("Crawl *under* the table," "Put your foot *in* your shoe."). Later let your child use an object ("Put the dog *between* the box and the scarf.").

Play *Simon Says.*

Play the see game: "I see _____ (something red). Can you find it?"

Use card games similar to "Old Maid," and make pairs by color, shape, animals, textures, or activities.

Play the plural game. Show your child a picture of a single object, then two or more pictures of the same object. (Dog, dogs; apple, apples.) Use only words that make plurals by adding an *s* (for instance, don't use *mouse* and *mice*).

Play the negation game: "This is a pig. It is not a _____ (goat)."

Play the discrimination game. At first use only one variable (color *or* shape): "Hand me the blue car. Hand me the blue comb." As your child develops this skill, use two variables (color *and* shape): "Hand me the blue triangle. Hand me the red square."

Play the why game: "Why do we _____(wear shoes . . ., take a nap . . ., go to church . . ., have trees in our yard)?"

Play the inside-outside game. Show your child some pictures or objects and ask where they belong—inside or outside the house.

Listening Activities

Point to various parts of your child's body and ask him to name them; as a variation, you can name the body parts and have your child point to them.

Use words in a short series and let your child repeat them; also use nonsense words to sharpen your child's hearing and speaking skills.

When you're going to do something different, explain the procedure to your child using the appropriate new words; then let him use the new words to gain understanding.

Instead of correcting your child's mispronunciation or inability to say a word, use it correctly yourself in a sentence.

Read stories to your child and encourage his verbalization.

Make sounds out of your child's sight (or even play a tape), and then let your child guess what the sounds are. Be sure to use familiar sounds, such as brushing teeth, beating eggs, a ringing telephone, or a barking dog.

Blindfold your child and let him count how many times you clap, bounce a ball, or hit a drum.

Let your child listen to various musical instruments—piano, radio, record, tape, guitar, horns.

Most times use your child's name when addressing him (do *not* use "son," "honey," or nicknames). He likes to be called by name.

Record your child's voice and play it back for him.

Discuss with your child his activities during the day to familiarize him with past, present, and future tenses.

Use descriptive words and examples (such as slick, rough, elastic, dissolve, transparent) when you talk to your child, and listen to his descriptive words. You'll probably like your child's better than yours!

Read your child appropriate poetry; he will love it!

Show your child pictures of things that sound alike (key-bee; car-star; ship-shoe; tree-train) and let your child name the things and point to them, or select the one you say.

Give simple instructions (using a puppet makes it more fun) and let your child carry them out (not more than two at a time at first): "Stand on one foot and then blink." "Sparky says for you to stick out your tongue and then jump."

You be a good listener when your child is talking.

Speaking Activities

Ask your child to describe certain activities, such as dressing or going to the store.

When your child gives unusual or inaccurate information about something, ask him for further explanation before you say that he is wrong.

Show your child something exciting; then let him examine, question, and discuss it.

Take your child on field trips (to the zoo, fire station, or museum). Listen and respond to his questions and comments.

Tell your child the correct names of objects and let him repeat them.

Help your child recite nursery rhymes.

Take a shoebox and make a small peek hole in one end. Inside the box place small pictures and objects. Let your child peek into the box and describe what he sees.

Let your child make up his own stories. Maybe you could help with some visual aids—they could be either made by the child or cut from magazines.

Give your child experience in asking and answering *wh* questions (what, why, when, and where).

Name or show a piece of furniture and ask your child what you do with it and where it belongs.

Make a "television" out of a large cardboard box and let your child dramatize from inside it.

Fabrics of different textures could be mounted on cardboard or wood. Let your child feel and describe the various materials.

Let your child tell you what he likes to do, has done, or would like to do.

Pay close attention when your child talks to you. Be a good listener.

Expand your child's sentences. If he says, "Me go," say, "You want to go"; if he says, "Dolly cry," you say, "The dolly is crying."

Reading Readiness

Introduction

There is evidence of children learning to read in the early preschool years. It can be done, but with the child so busy adjusting to his environment and his body, developing motor skills, and gaining autonomy and independence, he shouldn't be pressured into reading. Later, in school, reading will take more precedence. If he shows signs of interest, however, you can assist, but don't initiate or force reading. Because they think reading is the most important part of education, some people are mistakenly teaching a child to read too early in the child's development.

Preparation for Reading

You can lay a good foundation in the preschool years for later reading. First, read in your child's presence and show him that you enjoy it; then he will desire to read later, and will think reading is a pleasant experience. But if you ignore your child while *you* read or if you force a reluctant child to listen to or read stories, he will dread reading or will view it as a punishment.

Second, have appropriate books around for browsing, and be willing to read them out loud. Exposure to books under relaxed circumstances stimulates your child to want to learn to read. Children from homes where books are *not* available are at a disadvantage; they don't have the experience with the shapes of words and letters that is needed for successfully starting to read.

Third, read to your child only when you can *both* enjoy it. The warmth of your body nearby, your undivided attention, and a good book make a combination that is hard to beat. But when the child is engaged in other interests, when you are rushed, or when you dislike the book, he won't like reading with you.

Fourth, help lengthen your child's attention span by providing stimulating activities that interest him. Sustained activity is important, because reading takes concentration and time.

Fifth, help your child become aware of the left-right sequence used in reading (see *Bilateral Development* in Chapter One). Some people claim that well-established concepts of left and right in the child's body transfer to correct perceptual dimensions in visual space, specifically to discriminating such letters as *d-b*, *p-g*, and words such as *on-no* (Kephart in Cratty 1970), but convincing evidence is scarce (Cratty 1970). Letter—and even number—reversals are common in children until the age of seven. It has been suggested that letter rotations or reversals are the result of inexperience rather than of poor or slow physiological maturation (Lillie 1975).

Your child will be very interested in what all those little marks on the pages say about the pictures, and he may even ask about letters on boxes, on signs, or wherever there are written symbols. On a trip to the grocery store, Betty refused to put a certain box of cereal in the grocery cart because "that isn't the way they spell it on TV." Bruce, a four-year-old, and his mother were reading a book, a present given to him from a nearly blind grandmother. The book had been selected because of the charming animal pictures and not for the written message. Because it was in French, Bruce's mother had difficulty reading the book. Periodically Bruce selected the book, and his mother attempted to keep the dialogue consistent. On one such reading, Bruce said, "That isn't right. That word starts with a '*b*'. Read it like you did last time."

The preschooler will also want tools to practice writing, even though his letters will be crude and inconsistent. Asking about letters and trying to duplicate them are both indications of interest in reading. Be sure to introduce both capital and lowercase letters to your child. Take the time to answer his questions, even though it means repeating some answers again and again.

Reading readiness is a developmental process *within* your child. It is prefaced by maturation, meaningful experiences, and feelings of security. Watch your child carefully, and when *he* shows signs of being ready to read, try to help. Get professional guidance if necessary, but let your *child* be the leader (not you!), and you be the follower. In the meantime, provide the kinds of experiences that will sharpen your child's skills and that will provide a rich background for future learning. Don't try to teach reading if you don't know what you're doing: you could cause your preschooler problems when he gets into school, where unlearning and relearning will be a frustrating, disappointing, and time-consuming experience.

Help your child look forward to learning to read by giving him some fun, successful experiences with books and other activities. But try to avoid overexpectation. One kindergartener returned home from her first day of school; her face was long, and her disappointment was evident. Upon entering the house she declared, "I am never going to school again. That dumb teacher didn't even teach us how to read today." (It just so happens that this kindergartener had been hiding behind the couch reading her older sisters' books since she was three years old and now she thought her reading was going to become legitimate!)

Activities to Stimulate Reading Readiness

As the child gains skills and experiences, he will increase in the prerequisites for reading (longer interest span, greater concentration and interest, more attention to details, and a desire for knowledge).

Because sound discrimination is so important in reading, the reader is referred to the *Hearing (Auditory Perception)* discussion and activities in this chapter.

Activities Teaching the Use of Symbols

Let your child match cards that have the same letters, numbers, or designs.

Provide a model and let your child trace letters in sand, with fingerpaint, with utensils, or with fingers on textured letters made out of felt or sandpaper.

Take your child to the library or local bookmobile often. Let him help select some books to take home.

Make some kind of stiff board (using cardboard, blackboard, or sheets of heavy paper) for your child to write or draw on. A "tummy board" is handy.

Play games with your child, emphasizing sounds (beginning, middle, ending, rhyming). "I had a dog, his name was Abel. I found him sitting under the _____."

Get pairs of pictures of things that sound alike (sleep, sheep; bear, hair; clock, sock; stool, spool; hand, band). Say one of the words, and have your child choose the matching picture.

In a sack or box, have objects or pictures that contain certain letter sounds or combinations (*th*imble, *th*ree, *th*read, fea*th*er, and too*th*brush; *r*abbit, *r*adish, and *r*adio; *ch*urch, *ch*imney, *ch*in, and *ch*air). Let your child name each picture as he draws it from the container.

Help your child learn that written words are symbols. For example: talk with him about various body activities such as clapping, stamping, or turning. Design a symbol for each activity (an outline of a hand for clapping, a shoe for stamping, or a circle for turning around). Then assist in making a sequence of these symbols, such as hand, hand, shoe, circle, shoe, shoe, circle, hand. Let your child do as the symbols indicate: clap twice, stamp, turn around, stamp twice, turn around, clap. (This is kind of an introduction to international symbols such as road signs, restrooms, and so on.)

Let your child stack and place nesting cubes to exercise his visual discrimination of size.

Make some shadows of familiar objects and see if your child can guess what they are from their outlines.

After your child draws a picture, encourage him to tell you about it while you write his response on the paper.

Place a number of objects on a table or throughout the room. As you name each object, have your child point to it.

Show your child an object and ask him to find something in the room that rhymes with it (shell, bell; bee, key; moon, spoon).

Point to and say the name of an object that has the same sound beginning as another (*sh*ell, *sh*oe; *k*ey, *c*ar; *m*oon, *m*an). This activity will be more difficult, so say the harder one first so that your child can say the more familiar or easier one.

Let your child dictate stories into a tape recorder and listen to his own voice.

Put some signs on important things around the house (such as the toy box or bed).

Place pictures of clothing on the front of each drawer of your child's chest of drawers to show where each item of clothing belongs. Then your child can put away and find his own clothes.

Put your child's name on his things (clothes, bed, toys).

Show your child pictures of things with missing parts and ask him to identify the missing part (an airplane without a wing, a human body without an arm, an animal body without a leg, a face without a nose, a house without a door).

Point out signs in the community and tell your child what they say or mean.

Print your child's name (or other words). Give him a box of letters to select those that match. (Use both capital and lowercase letters.)

From a variety of corks and rubber tips, let your child place the right cork in each tip and then line them up by size. (You could also use nuts and bolts or nails in different-sized holes.)

Put a small object in each of several baby food or small glass jars. Have corresponding pictures of the objects for your child to match.

Make outlines of objects in cardboard. Let your child select and place the right object over its outline.

Given a variety of locks and keys (either attached to a board or in a box), let your child select the right key and open each lock.

See also *Activities for Left-Right Development.*

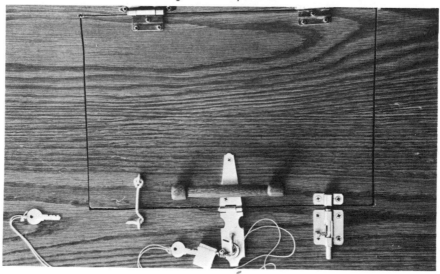

Math Skills

Developing Positive Attitudes Toward Math

As the family went for an outing in the car, Louise leaned forward from the back seat and asked her father, "Dad, how come the sign says 'four-zero,' and the red arrow on the car points to 'five-zero'?"

A ten-year-old was trying to make a financial gain by offering "five big orange coins for one small silver one." But his preschool brother remarked, "No, sir, I can buy a package of gum with this. All you can get for those big coins is round gum."

As illustrated by the above examples, the preschool child knows only a little about math, but he *will* be curious about numbers. Your preschool child lacks ability to think in abstract terms, and may even have trouble counting accurately at times. To force experiences involving concepts of quantity on your child can be a frustrating experience for all involved.

The best preparation for math begins with developing your child's visual skills. Sight appears to be more important for success in math than it does in reading (Brophy 1975), so your child needs opportunities to develop good sight, good eye-hand coordination, and the ability to make number discriminations. He may have trouble with math if numbers are perceived incorrectly.

Don't shudder every time you hear the word *math*—even if you were a poor math student or have frustrating experiences like never being able to balance the budget or alter measurements for cooking, sewing, or building. Your remarks could discourage your child, making his job of mastering math skills a lot more difficult. On the other hand, if you were a genius in math, you may not be able to understand why your child can't grasp concepts more rapidly. But remember to have patience; he will eventually understand.

Preparing Your Child for Math Skills

Your child needs lots of good, firsthand experiences: to learn to count, to use counting for important reasons, and to see other uses (such as phone and house numbers) for numbers. Although you might be tempted to try to help him by using a clock with animals or pictures instead of numbers, you wouldn't really be helping. How would it be if your child came to you and said, "The big hand is on the cow, and the little hand is on the tree"? He would get more real help if you used a standard clock; then your child could say, "The big hand is on the four and the little hand is on the nine." Numbers are then associated with time.

Your preschool child can learn cardinal numbers (numbers that show amount, such as 2, 147, or 216) and ordinal numbers (numbers that indicate position, such as first, tenth, twelfth). But it's better to associate numbers with his experiences instead of just teaching him to recite them from memory. He will want to learn to count, but don't get upset over mistakes. Remember that up to now your child has learned to count only a few numbers, perhaps aided by using his fingers. As the two of you do things that are conducive to counting, try to count spontaneously: "One, two, three carrots." "First your shirt, second your pants."

Learning ordinal numbers comes from learning relationships within a group. Your child will learn that to be "first" is great, but he will have to learn to tolerate other positions—even last. Give some simple definitions: first means *before* any others; last means *after* all others.

You can help your child develop some goals in mathematics by stimulating his interest in numbers. Show how numbers can help in problem solving (how many objects he needs), how they are used in the everyday world (recipes), and how number symbols can replace words (phone numbers and addresses). Your child can probably do simple addition in instances where you provide one item, like a cookie, for each person: "We need a cookie for John, and Sara, and Daddy, and me." Before the preschool years end, your child will be able to count the people, know the number needed, and then count the needed items— rather than to provide things on a one-to-one correspondence, as he did before.

Another way to help your child learn about numbers is by exploring measuring units: cups, spoons, tapes, and rulers. "I have to fill the white cup twice to fill the green one once." "The tape has to be this long to measure how tall I am." "It takes the same length of string to measure me when I stand up as when I sit down!"

You can introduce basic mathematical terms to your child as long as you define them and give experiences with them: "We don't have enough cups. We need to *add,* or get, more." "We have too many cards. We need to *subtract,* or take away, some." In these two instances, *more* and *some* do *not* denote a certain quantity. Don't use them too often, or your child may think they *do* represent a certain number. Words like *more, some,* and *less* are confusing and will often be used interchangeably by your child.

There has been a shift to *new* math, perhaps recently a shift away from it. Now all of us are challenged to learn the metric system. In many instances, parents and preschoolers will start out on about the same level. You'll both need to be encouraged, have positive attitudes, and forge ahead.

Activities for Stimulating Math Skills

Learning math is one of the more difficult tasks for the preschooler. He will make only a small dent in it, but there are lots of fun things you can do together to stimulate interest.

Measuring and Counting Activities

Let your child experiment with measuring spoons and cups, scales, and weights.

Give your child a tape measure, a yardstick, a metal tape, or some string and let him measure various things.

Ask a shoe salesman to measure your child's foot, and then show your child the right size of shoe.

Show your child how you use a recipe to make something for dinner.

Weigh and measure your child often, and record his growth.

Help your child measure the ingredients and make something for creative use—clay, paste, or fingerpaint, for example. (See recipe section.)

Let your child measure with sticks (twelve one-inch sticks equal a one-foot ruler; three one-foot rulers equal one yardstick).

Teach your child the concept of zero as well as the numbers: "One button on a card, two buttons on a card. But when we take them all off, we have zero (or no) buttons left."

Make an egg carton counter. In the lid, place small cards with pictures of from zero to six objects on each card. Write corresponding numbers on the egg carton sections. Let your child take the pictures and place them in the appropriately numbered sections.

Help your child put the appropriate number of candles on a cake for every birthday.

Let your child set the table using the appropriate number of utensils.

Have your child match dominoes.

Encourage your child to sort things into number piles: one stick in the first pile, two sticks in the second pile, and so on.

Make a number board with a piece of wood, nails, and washers. One washer fits over a short nail; two washers fit over a longer nail; and so on, up to five. Your child puts the correct number of washers on each nail.

Sing counting songs: "Ten Little Indians," "This Old Man," and "One, Two, Buckle My Shoe."

Teach fingerplays that use numbers or that label fingers as to size.

Write a number symbol on one side and a corresponding number of dots on the opposite side of each of several baby food jars. Let your child put the correct number of beans, pennies, objects, or marbles in each jar.

Let your child have some experiences with a thermometer (put it in various places in the house, such as the refrigerator, or use it in making candy) and see how it changes.

Show your child how to dial the telephone and to call someone he knows.

Let your child help you fill the car with gas at the service station. Show him how much gas is needed, and let him pay for it.

Get a coin bank that your child can see into. Each week give him a small allowance or some earned money to put in the bank.

Help your child make a picture recipe that he could follow.

Combining and Calendar Activities

Cut shapes from heavy cardboard, tagboard, or wood for your child to put together to make larger shapes (one-half circles, one-quarter circles, triangles, oblongs, or wedges).

Provide blocks for experience with geometric shapes.

Help your child make a mobile (an experience in balance).

Let your child stack blocks by size or shape.

Show your child on a calendar how many days there are until a certain event (do not have this activity too far in advance of the event, because it is so hard to wait). Cut the numbers off of the calendar, and let your child place them on another ruled sheet or calendar as the days go by.

Make a large monthly calendar to hang on the wall. Make corresponding individual numbers for each day and place them in a box. Each day help your child match the date with a number in the box and then attach it to the calendar.

Give your child various parts of an object and let him assemble it (smaller blocks combined to make a larger object; slices of apple to make a whole apple).

Games to Play

When your child can name number symbols and count, play games that have dice (or one die) or a number spinner.

Make up a number game. Give your child some instructions involving numbers (ask him to get six oranges or three flowers), and see if he can accurately follow the directions.

Play *Give and Take*. Both of you start with the same number of objects; tell your child to give or take a certain number, and then he tells you to make another exchange.

Play *Equal*. There are at least three ways to play: (1) Show your child how to put the same number of objects on each side of an equal sign (three bananas on this side and three bananas on the other side). (2) With coins pasted on a cardboard, show your child that ten pennies are the same as (equal to) one dime (or five for one nickel). Be careful with this method, because it may be too advanced. (3) Using a scale, show your child how to balance it by putting the same weight on each side. You put objects in one container, and let him put objects in the other container until they balance.

Language Activities

Point out number symbols from the environment (mileage signs and speedometer, temperature and weather) to your child, and explain their meaning.

Teach the numbers one through five (or ten, if your child is ready).

Clap, bounce a ball, or ring a bell, and let your child count the number of times you do it.

Count similar objects while looking at books or pictures.

Point out number symbols in things you buy at the store (boxes, bottles).

Help your child learn the names of various coins.

Point out your house number and help your child learn his address and phone number.

Point out the number on a radio station or television channel.

Help your child count objects (buttons, marbles, cubes, pegs, people).

Show your child how stopwatches, clocks, and watches work.

Help your child make a time schedule for a special event (a birthday party or trip).

Help your child compare sizes of things—blocks, shapes, clothes.

Give your child experiences with concepts like *longer* or *shorter, heavier* or *lighter,* and other opportunities in measurement.

Read books that teach number concepts.

Media and Learning

Visual Aids in Learning

Media is a very important part of education, especially during the preschool years. The child really *does* learn better when visual aids are presented than when they're not presented, because he can involve a number of his senses—seeing, hearing, feeling, and often smelling and tasting. The visual aids should be clear, accurate, and uncluttered, but they don't have to be in color. It is imperative that media stimulate and aid the child (suggest ideas or questions or invite involvement), but that they not stifle or alienate him (be too abstract or nontouchable).

Television

There are some very good things about television. You can see things on television that you could never see in person: a closeup of a cow chewing her cud, shots inside cages at the zoo, or a trip to the ocean might be too frightening (or even impossible) for a young child, but on television they can be very interesting if the young child is kept in mind. Special programs that have been edited for young children—programs that are short, simple, attractive, and entertaining—are needed. They don't have to be fictional—real things are exciting and mind-broadening for preschoolers. When the two of you sit down and enjoy a program together, your child can ask you questions about puzzling ideas or can just talk about what he sees. These discussions help him interpret new information about the world.

By the age of eighteen, if your child is average, he will have spent more time in front of the television than in any other single activity except sleep (Liebert and Baron 1972). Don't you think this fact deserves your careful attention? You may think your child is not paying attention to television, but chances are you're wrong. Also consider this information: ninety-six percent of American homes have at least one television set, the television is on for an average of six hours a day in every home, and most children start watching television for two hours a day when they are only two or three years old. *TV Guide* sells more copies than does any other magazine in the country, and a sixteen-year-old has spent as many hours in front of the television set as he has in school. You need to consider whether television makes the best use of your child's time.

Television viewing also has an impact on family interaction. Sometimes watching television is the only time families spend together, but it is a poor substitute for having a social activity or for building interpersonal relationships. Some mothers actually think that childrearing is easier now than it was in pre-television days because children roughhouse less and bother parents with fewer questions (Garbarino 1972). These mothers don't stop to think about the absence of physical, mental, or social development in their children's lives. Children may even become lazy or uninterested in reading because reading is more work than watching television.

Television also feeds children distorted ideas as to male and female roles. When trying to analyze sex-role description in the ten most popular commercially produced children's shows, researchers had to omit four because *no* female characters appeared in them. Males were aggressive, constructive, and they played a variety of roles; but females, when present, were ignored, given minor parts, or even punished when their behavior became active. (Being a *witch* seemed to be almost the only female role, and it was portrayed in four out of the five female lead characters.) Even the commercials (1,241 of them) showed women only inside the home, while men's activities ranged from politics to fishing. A small three-tenths of one percent (0.3%) of the commercials in this study showed women as "autonomous, independent people" (Papalia and Olds 1975). How can children develop any kind of accurate sex-role identification when television gives this kind of "help"?

Television sets are often on too much, so children watch them instead of playing outside, learning to get along with others, or developing the important art of conversation. Peer group interaction may actually be hampered by so much television.

Another problem with television is that reality and fantasy often overlap. Saturday morning cartoons have many events that the young child doesn't understand—how somebody can die and come right back to life (when people really don't), how animals can talk, sing, and do other things, why everybody has to be hitting and fighting, why there is so much loud noise, and why the music is so awful. Children should be actively playing in the real world, not passively sitting in a fantasy land. Television can inhibit children from self-initiating ideas; it also actually reduces their creativity (Education U.S.A. 1973).

Have you heard the story about the couple who decided not to have a television set because they didn't want their children exposed to "those awful" programs and "bad" influences, plus they *did* want their children to do all those "creative" (art, music, literature) and "good" things (physical activity, reading, interpersonal relationship building)? Well, it just happened that their young schoolage child was continually bribing neighbor children with favors and objects so he could go into their homes and watch television; he'd even call up early on non-school days to watch television. But the straw that broke the camel's back was early one "sleep-in" morning when neighboring parents woke up with the child in their bedroom watching cartoons! Or there's the story about the parents who came home one evening to find their six- and nine-year-old boys watching a television program. Upon inquiring about the plot of the program, the boys freely volunteered that "that man had raped that girl and now she can't have any more babies!"

A group of Boston mothers (Action for Children's Television) recently objected to the number of commercials aired during toddler-aimed shows, especially on Saturday morning. They complained that up to *three times* as many commercials were shown during this time as they were during adult shows, and they petitioned the Federal Communications Commission to remove commercials during children's programs. These mothers realized that it is sometimes hard to tell where the programs stop and the commercials begin. When a child sees commercials on television about how good products are or what they can help him do, he is pretty persuasive in getting parents to buy—even if the commercials are misleading. The child tends to believe everything seen and heard—including the commercials.

Another problem with television is that it is geared to general viewing. It is not adapted to individual needs or readiness. Misconceptions can arise that aren't cleared up; there is no time for questions, discussion, or repetition. Ideas only partially understood do *not* add to learning. The child may be bewildered and overwhelmed by the excitement, speed, noise, and constantly changing stimuli on television. The child needs the world presented in small enough doses of actual, real-life experiences. *You* know what is fact and what is fantasy, but *he* doesn't—not until the age of five or six can most children sort out some of the real and the fantasy. Currently there are children sustaining injuries from imitating superhuman qualities they have seen on television programs.

You should also consider the problem of television violence affecting children. So much violence on television makes the child feel it is all right for him to do the same thing; but then he gets punished for hitting someone. Although violence may give an adult a chance to drain off some hostility or aggressive feelings by watching, it only intensifies violence in the young child. His impulses are strong; he wants to bite or kick or hurt, but television doesn't help him bring these feelings under control or provide acceptable outlets (words or constructive activities) for aggressive feelings.

Sometimes the young child can be really frightened by some of the violence on television—whether it involves human characters or characters in cartoons. Violent human actions stay in his mind very vividly (Osborn and Endsley 1971). The child is much more willing to engage in aggression if he sees an aggressive program than if he sees a neutral program (Liebert and Baron 1972).

Because there has been so much controversy about television violence for young children, a committee was established to study it. But the three major networks had veto power over the committee members; individuals who had spoken sharply about television violence were omitted from the committee, and most of the members were from commercial television. At best, their results were misleading; they failed to report a correlation between television violence and viewer aggression that had been "impressively strong and remarkably consistent" in the study (Liebert and Baron 1972).

At present the Parent-Teacher Association is conducting a nationwide survey on the impact television (especially violence) has upon children and youth. The results of this year-long study can be used as a basis for later change.

Sometimes educational television isn't much better than commercial television. Some of their programs are pretty good, but many programs for young children were started because of adult anxieties and adult politics—not because of needs in children's growth and development, the need for actual experiences, the need to strengthen feelings of autonomy or initiative, or the need for sound personality development. The best way for a child to develop language skills is through active conversation with others, not by listening to words and ideas that are too hard to understand at a speed that is too fast to comprehend or to allow for questions (Read 1976).

Movies and Books

The movies also want to get your attention—and your money. Some of them are interesting, but most of the time they are long and boring and even frightening for the young child. Just because a certain name appears on a movie, don't be misled: very few movies are actually appropriate for preschool children. Do you realize how frightening it can be to see an animal, like Bambi, lost from its mother, or to see a raging fire, or to watch a car go through the air? The young child thinks the witch in *Snow White* is actually giving that poisonous apple to *him*. The child identifies with Snow White, and the witch is a frightening, ugly old lady. If you want to take your child to a movie, go to one where there are *real* animals and people doing real things. These are the best ones for the young child to relate to.

Criteria for Evaluating Media

Many of the above comments about television and movies also apply to books and stories. Good criteria for selecting media materials for the young child are as follows: They should (1) be realistic, accurately reported, and interesting; (2) be entertaining and humorous for the child; (3) promote firsthand experiences; (4) be on the child's developmental level of understanding; (5) have a plot with positive effects on the child; (6) have interesting words and sounds and direct conversation; (7) help increase the child's knowledge; and (8) be consistent—the written or spoken text and the visuals should support each other. (For further information, see Taylor 1975.)

References for Adults

Cognitive Development:

Bloom, B., *Stability and Change in Human Characteristics,* New York: Wiley, 1964.

Brophy, Jere E., Thomas L. Good, and Shari E. Nedler, *Teaching in the Pre-school,* New York: Harper and Row Publishers, 1975.

Bruner, Jerome, *Toward a Theory of Instruction,* Cambridge, Mass.: Harvard University Press, 1966.

Carmichael, V., *Science Experiences for Young Children,* Los Angeles: Southern California Association for the Education of Young Children, 1969.

Carson, R., *The Sense of Wonder,* New York: Harper and Row Publishers, 1956.

Estvan, F. J., "The Social Perception of Nursery School Children," *Elementary School Journal,* 66: 1966, 7.

Gill, N., T. Herdtner, and L. Lough, "Perceptual and Socioeconomic Variables, Instruction in Body-Orientation and Predicted Academic Success in Young Children," *Perceptual and Motor Skills,* 26: 1968, 1175–84.

Hendrick, J., *The Whole Child: New Trends in Early Education,* St. Louis: The C. V. Mosby Company, 1975.

Hunt, J., *Intelligence and Experience,* New York: Ronald, 1961.

Hurlock, E., *Child Development,* New York: McGraw-Hill, 1972.

Lavatelli, C. S., *Early Childhood Curriculum: A Piaget Program,* Boston: American Science and Engineering, Inc., 1970 (a).

Lavatelli, C. S., *Piaget's Theory Applied to an Early Childhood Curriculum,* Boston: American Science and Engineering, Inc., 1970 (b).

Lillie, D. L., *Early Childhood Education,* Chicago: Science Research Associates, Inc., 1975.

Lugo, J., and H. L. Hershey, *Human Development,* New York: Macmillan Publishing Company, 1974.

Neuman, D., "Sciencing for Young Children," in K. R. Read, ed., *Ideas That Work with Young Children,* Washington, D.C.: NAEYC, 1972.

Roeper, A., and I. E. Sigel, "Finding the Clue to Children's Thought Processes," in Hartup, W. W., and Nancy L. Smothergill, eds., *The Young Child,* Washington, D.C.: NAEYC, 1967, pp. 77–95.

Rohwer, W., "Implications of Cognitive Development for Education," in P. Mussen, ed., *Carmichael's Manual of Child Development,* third edition, volume 1, New York: Wiley, 1970.

Rohwer, W., "Images and Pictures in Children's Learning: Research Results and Educational Implications," *Psychological Bulletin* 73 (1970), pp. 393–403.

Sharp, E., *Thinking Is Child's Play,* New York: E. P. Dutton and Company, Inc., 1969.

Sigel, L. S., "Development of the Concept of Seriation," *Developmental Psychology,* 1972, 6, pp. 135–137.

Smart, M., and R. C. Smart, *Preschool Children: Development and Relationships,* New York: Macmillan, 1973.

Stern, V., *The Role of Play in Cognitive Development,* Final Report, Research Division, New York: Bank Street College of Education, 1973.

Stevenson, H., "Learning in Children," in P. Mussen, ed., *Carmichael's Manual of Child Psychology,* third edition, volume 1, New York: Wiley, 1970.

Sutton-Smith, B., "The Role of Play in Cognitive Development," in Hartup, W.

W. and N. L. Smothergill, eds., *The Young Child*, Washington, D.C.: 1967, pp. 96–108.

Taylor, B. J., *A Child Goes Forth*, Provo, Utah: Brigham Young University Press, 1975.

Taylor, B. J., *When I Do, I Learn*, Provo, Utah: Brigham Young University Press, 1974.

Weikart, D. P., L. Rogers, C. Adcock, and D. McClelland, *The Cognitively Oriented Curriculum: A Framework for Preschool Teachers*, Washington, D.C.: NAEYC, 1971.

Sense Perception:

Brophy, J. E., T. L. Good, and S. E. Nedler, *Teaching in the Preschool*, New York: Harper and Row Publishers, 1975.

Cratty, B. J., *Perceptual and Motor Development in Infants and Children*, New York: Macmillan, 1970.

Frostig, M., and D. Horne, *The Frostig Program for the Development of Visual Perception*, Chicago: Follett, 1964.

Hurlock, Elizabeth, *Child Development*, New York: McGraw-Hill, 1972.

Lillie, David L., *Early Childhood Education*, Chicago: Science Research Associates, Inc., 1975.

Lugo, J. O., and H. L. Hershey, *Human Development*, New York: Macmillan, 1974.

Montagu, Ashley, *Touching: The Human Significance of the Skin*, New York: Columbia University Press, 1971.

Smart, M., and R. C. Smart, *Preschool Children: Development and Relationships*, New York: Macmillan, 1973.

Divergent Thinking:

Estvan, F. J., "Teaching the Very Young: Procedures for Developing Inquiry Skills," in R. H. Anderson and H. G. Shane, eds., *As the Twig Is Bent: Readings in Early Childhood Education*, New York: Houghton Mifflin Company, 1971.

Guilford, J. P., *The Nature of Human Intelligence*, New York: McGraw-Hill Book Company, 1967.

Lieberman, J. N., "Playfulness and Divergent Thinking Ability: an Investigation of Their Relationship at the Kindergarten Level," in M. Almy, ed., *Early Childhood Play: Selected Readings Related to Cognition and Motivation*, New York: Simon and Schuster, Inc., 1968.

Meeker, M. N., *The Structure of Intellect: Its Interpretation and Uses*, Columbus, Ohio: Charles E. Merrill Publishing Company, 1969.

Sutton-Smith, B., "A Syntax for Play and Games," in R. E. Herron and B. Sutton-Smith, eds., *Child's Play*, New York: John Wiley and Sons, Inc., 1971.

Language Use and Development:

Belgau, F., *A Motor Perceptual Development Handbook of Activities for Schools, Parents and Preschool Programs*, LaPorte, Texas: Perception Development Research Associates, 1967.

Brophy, Jere E., Thomas L. Good, and Shari E. Nedler, *Teaching in the Preschool*, New York: Harper and Row Publishers, 1975.

Cazden, C. B., *Language in Early Childhood Education*, Washington, D.C.: NAEYC, 1972.

Engle, R. C., *Language Motivating Experiences for Young Children*, Van Nuys, Calif.: DFA Publishers, 1968.

Hendrick, Joanne, *The Whole Child: New Trends in Early Education,* St. Louis: The C. V. Mosby Company, 1975.

Holt, John, *How Children Learn,* New York: Dell Publishing Company, Inc., 1967.

Hurlock, Elizabeth, *Child Development,* New York: McGraw-Hill, 1972.

Karnes, M. B., *Helping Young Children Develop Language Skills: A Book of Activities,* Washington, D.C.: Council for Exceptional Children, 1968.

Lewis, M. M., *Language, Thought and Personality,* New York: Basic Books, Inc., 1963.

Lichtenberg, P., and D. G. Norton, *Cognitive and Mental Development in the First Five Years of Life: a Review of Recent Research,* Rockville, Md.: National Institutes of Mental Health, 1970.

Lillie, David L., *Early Childhood Education,* Chicago: Science Research Associates, Inc., 1975.

Lugo, James O. and Herald L. Hershey, *Human Development,* New York: Macmillan Publishing Company, Inc., 1974.

McCarthy, D., "Language Development in Children," in L. Carmichael, ed., *Manual of Child Psychology,* 2nd ed., New York: John Wiley and Sons, Inc., 1954.

Masland, Mary Wooton, *Learning to Talk: Speech, Hearing and Language Problems in the Pre-School Child,* Developed by the National Institute of Neurological Diseases and Stroke, Washington, D.C.: U.S. Department of Health, Education, and Welfare, 1969.

Menyuk, P., "Syntactic Structures in the Language of Children," *Child Development,* 1963, 34, 407–422.

Ryan, S., A. Hegion, and J. Flavell, "Nonverbal Mnemonic Mediation in Preschool Children," mimeographed report, Minneapolis: University of Minnesota, 1969.

Scott, Louise Binder, *Learning Time with Language Experiences for Young Children,* San Francisco: McGraw Hill, 1968.

Smart, Mollie, and Russell C. Smart, *Preschool Children: Development and Relationships,* New York: Macmillan, 1973.

Sutton-Smith, B., *Child Psychology,* Englewood Cliffs, N.J.: Prentice-Hall, 1973.

Reading Readiness:

Coyte, Rhoda J., *Simple Sequential Procedures in the Teaching of Word Attack Skills,* Provo, Utah: Brigham Young University Publications, 1971.

Cratty, B. J., *Perceptual and Motor Development in Infants and Children,* New York: Macmillan, 1970.

DeHirsch, J., J. Jansky, and W. Langford, *Predicting Reading Failure,* New York: Harper and Row, 1966.

Durkin, Dolores, *Teaching Them to Read,* Boston: Allyn and Bacon, 1970.

Gill, N., T. Herdtner, and L. Lough, "Perceptual and Socioeconomic Variables, Instruction in Body-Orientation, and Predicted Academic Success in Young Children," *Perceptual and Motor Skills,* 26: 1968, 1175–84.

Hafner, L. E., and H. B. Jolly, *Patterns of Teaching Reading in the Elementary School,* New York: Macmillan, 1972.

Heilman, A. W., *Principles and Practices of Teaching Reading,* Columbus, Ohio: Charles E. Merrill Book, 1961.

Herr, Selma E., *Learning Activities for Reading,* 2nd ed., Dubuque, Iowa: Wm. C. Brown Company, 1970.

Holt, J., *How Children Learn,* New York: Dell Publishing Company, Inc., 1967.

Hymes, J. L., Jr., *Before the Child Reads,* Evanston, Ill.: Row-Peterson, 1958.

Kahn, D., and H. Birch, "Development of Auditory/Visual Integration and Reading Achievement," *Perceptual and Motor Skills,* 27: 1968, 459–68.

Lazroe, J., "An Investigation of the Effects of Motor Training on the Reading Readiness of Kindergarten Children," *Dissertation Abstracts,* 29, 8 (1969), 2609a.

Leavitt, J. E., ed., *Nursery-Kindergarten Education,* New York: McGraw-Hill Book Company, Inc., 1958.

Lindberg, L., and R. Swedlow, *Early Childhood Education,* Boston: Allyn and Bacon, Inc., 1976.

Lorton, Mary Baratta, *Workjobs,* Menlo Park, Calif.: Addison-Wesley Publishing Company, 1973.

Monroe, M., and B. Rogers, *Foundations for Reading,* Glenview, Ill.: Scott, Foresman and Company, 1964.

Papp, H., "Visual Discrimination of Alphabetic Letters," *The Reading Teacher,* 1964, 17:221–25.

Rosner, J., *The Development and Validation of an Individualized Perceptual Skills Curriculum,* Pittsburgh: University of Pittsburgh, Learning Research and Development Center, 1972.

Scott, L. B., *Learning Time with Language Experiences for Young Children,* San Francisco: McGraw-Hill, 1968.

Winick, M. P., *Before the 3 R's,* New York: David McKay Company, 1973.

Math Skills:

Adkins, Dorothy C., et al., *Preschool Mathematics Curriculum Project,* Final Report, ERIC Document 038 168, November 1969, 28 pp.

Ashlock, Robert, "What Math for Fours and Fives?" *Childhood Education,* April 1967, p. 469.

Cahoon, Owen W., *A Teachers' Guide to Cognitive Tasks for Preschool,* Provo, Utah: Brigham Young University Press, 1974.

Carmichael, Viola S., *Curriculum Ideas for Young Children,* Pasadena, Calif.: 1886 Kinneola Canyon Road, 91107.

Croft, Doreen J., and Robert D. Hess, *An Activities Handbook for Teachers of Young Children,* Boston: Houghton Mifflin Company, 1972, pp. 148–70.

Heard, Ida Mae, "Number Games with Young Children," *Young Children,* January 1969, pp. 147–50.

Heard, Ida Mae, "Mathematical Concepts and Abilities Possessed by Kindergarten Entrants," *Arithmetic Teacher* 17:4 (1970), pp. 340–41.

Hildebrand, V., *Introduction to Early Childhood Education,* New York: Macmillan Company, 1971, pp. 163–65.

Hucklesby, Sylvia, *Opening Up the Classroom: A Walk Around the School,* University of Illinois, Urbana, Ill.: ERIC Clearinghouse on Early Childhood Education, 1971.

Leeper, Sarah H., Ruth J. Dales, Dora S. Skipper, and Ralph L. Witherspoon, *Good Schools for Young Children,* New York: Macmillan Company, 1974, 3rd ed., pp. 234–58.

Maertens, N. W., "Who's Afraid of Modern Math?" *Parents' Magazine,* August, 1971.

Mills, Belen, ed., *Understanding the Young Child and His Curriculum,* New York: Macmillan Company, 1972, pp. 344–46 (bibliography and selected readings).

Rea, R. E., and R. E. Reys, "Mathematics Competence of Entering Kindergarteners," *Arithmetic Teacher* 17:1 (1970), pp. 701–05.

Rosner, J., *The Development and Validation of an Individualized Perceptual Skills Curriculum,* Pittsburgh: University of Pittsburgh, Learning Research and Development Center, 1972.

Spodek, B., *Teaching in the Early Years,* Englewood Cliffs, N.J.: Prentice-Hall, 1972, pp. 137–53. (Also see selected readings on page 153.)

Vance, Barbara, *Teaching the Prekindergarten Child,* Monterey, Calif.: Brooks/Cole Publishing Company, 1973, pp. 269–82.

Withers, Carl, *Counting Out Rhymes,* New York: Dover, 1970.

Media in Learning:

Action for Children's Television, New York: Discus Books/Avon, 1971.

Bronfenbrenner, Urie, ed., *Influences on Human Development,* Hinsdale, Ill.: The Dryden Press, Inc., 1972.

Cohen, Dorothy, "Is TV a Pied Piper?" *Young Children,* November, 1974.

Education U.S.A., University of Southern California, October 29, 1973.

Garbarino, J., "A Note on the Effects of Television Viewing," in Urie Bronfenbrenner, ed., *Influences on Human Development,* Hinsdale, Ill.: The Dryden Press, Inc., 1972, pp. 499–502.

Holden, Constance, "TV Violence: Government Study Yields More Evidence, No Verdict," in Urie Bronfenbrenner, ed., *Influences on Human Development,* Hinsdale, Ill.: The Dryden Press, Inc., 1972, pp. 494–499.

Liebert, Robert M. and Robert A. Baron, "Some Immediate Effects of Televised Violence on Children's Behavior," in Urie Bronfenbrenner, ed., *Influences on Human Development,* Hinsdale, Ill.: The Dryden Press, Inc., 1972, pp. 483–492.

Melody, W., *Children's TV: The Economics of Exploitation,* New Haven: Yale Press, 1973.

Osborn, D. K. and R. C. Endsley, "Emotional Reactions of Young Children to TV Violence," *Child Development,* 42, 1971, 321–331.

Papalia, D. E., and S. W. Olds, *A Child's World,* New York: McGraw-Hill, 1975.

Read, K., *The Nursery School,* 6th ed., Philadelphia: Saunders, 1976.

Taylor, B. J., "The Ability of Three-, Four-, and Five-Year-Olds to Distinguish Reality from Fantasy," *Jr. of Genetic Psychology* 122 (1973):315–18.

Taylor, B. J., *A Child Goes Forth* (revised edition), Provo, Utah: Brigham Young University Press, 1975.

Books for Children:

Sight or visual perception:
Showers, Paul and Kay, *Look at Your Eyes,* Crowell.
Taste perception:
Showers, Paul and Kay, *How Many Teeth?* Crowell; *How You Talk,* Crowell.
Smell or olfactory perception:
Schlein, Miriam, *Little Red Nose,* Abelard-Schuman, 1955.
Showers, Paul and Kay, *Follow Your Nose,* Crowell.
Touch or tactile perception:
Aliki, *My Five Senses,* Crowell, 1962.
Aliki, *My Hands.*
Gibson, Myra T., *What Is Your Favorite Thing to Touch?* New York: Grosset and Dunlap, Inc., 1965.
Showers, Paul and Kay, *Finding Out by Touching,* Crowell; *Your Skin and Mine,* Crowell, 1965.
Steiner, Charlotte, *My Bunny Feels Soft,* New York: Knopf, 1958.

Hearing or auditory perception:

Brown, Margaret W., *Sh-h-h-h, Bang,* Harper, 1943; *The Noisy Books,* Harper.

Branley, F. M., *High Sounds, Low Sounds,* Crowell, 1967.

Darby, Gene, *What Is a Sound?* Benefic Press.

Parker, Bertha M., *Sound,* Row, Peterson, 1953.

Podendorf, I., *The True Book of Sounds We Hear,* Children's Press, 1955, 1971.

Ryland, Lee, *Gordon and the Glockenspiel,* Whitman, 1961.

Showers, Paul and Kay, *The Listening Walk,* Crowell.

Steiner, Charlotte, *Kiki Loves Music,* Doubleday, 1949.

Wolff, Janet, *Let's Imagine Sounds,* Dutton, 1962.

Three

Emotional Development

A Note from Your Preschooler

Dear Mom and Dad,

Now that I am getting bigger, I can do more and more things by myself. I can wash my own hands and face. I can play one game longer and I can wait longer for things. I am willing to try harder things. I can even do jobs around the house and tell you how well I did. When you smile at me and tell me I can do new things, I really feel great.

But don't make me to do things I'm not big enough for. I feel bad when I can't do what you want.

Sometimes I want things that aren't good for me. I need you to show me what I can or can't do and tell me why. Yesterday when I was playing with Freddy I pushed him down, grabbed his toy, and ran. When he tried to get it back, I bit him. Then you came and made me give the toy back to him. I was so mad. Why couldn't you understand I wanted it so much I *had* to take it? Maybe you could have found me a toy that was almost as good. Or maybe you could have let me take a turn with his toy later.

I need things that help me get my feelings out from inside me. Running, hammering, pounding clay, and painting are fun. Pretending makes me feel big and strong, not little and weak. I can use *all* my feelings—even the bad ones. And I can mix real and pretend while I learn how things work. My friends and I can learn to do things together and we understand each other—both what we say and what we do. I can do big things and little things the way *I* want to. And I can learn how to be first and how to be second or third.

Please help me learn how to like myself. Then I can learn to do things by myself and be happy.

       Love,
       Your Preschooler

Introduction

The young child needs just the right amount of freedom, opportunity, structure, and support; too much or too little of any of these can be harmful. Outside pressure that does not match the preschooler's inner control is likely to make him angry or anxious. He needs discussions with adults who care, and chances to test his limits, but most of all he needs opportunities to experience things for himself and to receive responses from others. The more aware your child is of his own feelings and the better his ability to successfully handle (cope with) different situations, the more he will want and accept new experiences. Your child needs assurance and control in situations; you can play a very important role here.

Before the age of three or four, your child needs frequent and intense contact with you; but after four years of age, the need for such contact will decrease. Your child's dependency on you will be greater if you withdraw your love in disciplining your child, if you show him signs of rejection, if you punish direct aggression against yourself, or if you express your affection too much or overprotect your child (Smart and Smart 1973).

To build trust in others, your child needs to have his own basic needs met with consistency and satisfaction. He needs to explore, develop curiosity, and try new things.

You can greatly help your child's emotional development by accepting and liking yourself. The happier you are with yourself, the more you can help your child be happy with himself. If you are always concerned with *your* problems, you won't be able to recognize and help solve your child's problems.

Sometime preceding middle childhood, a person forms a general idea of his own worth. Interviews with mothers of high self-esteem children disclosed that the mothers gave nearly total acceptance of the child, set limits that were clearly defined and enforced, and showed respect for individual differences within guidelines. There was no rejection, ambiguity, disrespect, or harsh emotional punishment on the part of these mothers (Coopersmith 1967). Although it was expected that little structure and much freedom in the home environment would produce high self-esteem in children, researchers found the opposite: *restricted* freedom gave stability to the child. In other words, children who know and keep their limits develop greater self-esteem.

Your demands should be predictable and your punishment should be consistent. Rejection or punishment lower the child's self-esteem. Why should your child attempt anything if he knows it's impossible to please you? The chance of failure is so high. Your child needs to know that your love is unconditional; you may be disappointed at times, but if your preschooler knows that you're still accepting and loving, he will try again.

You should know what behavior you can reasonably expect at different stages of your child's development so that your child has the "opportunity for *real* but *manageable* responsibility" (Brophy 1975). For example, let your child make a mess under certain conditions (for instance, when a friend has come to play) if he is willing to clean the mess up. To help your child perform at an age-appropriate emotional level, you should expect him to conform to some basic routines. Your preschooler should be able to settle down, concentrate on, and get involved in play, but he should be able to express his feelings and ideas appropriately. You can help if you are consistent, reasonable, trustful, congruent, empathetic, and loving, while recognizing your child's indications of stress and frustration. When he is experiencing difficulty, step in and assist him before it is too late. Keep control of your emotions, be fair, and let the punishment fit the crime. By all means notice when your child does something *right,* and make favorable comments; doing so will work wonders.

Childrearing Approaches

Three major childrearing approaches have been identified as (1) power-assertive, where physical punishment, threats, and deprivation of privileges are the parent's main tools; (2) withdrawal of love, where parents ignore the child, refuse to listen to or speak to the child, or isolate him in a nonphysical manner; and (3) induction, a method whereby parents use explanation, discuss consequences, or appeal to the child's pride (Hoffman 1970). The power-assertive and love withdrawal methods are highly punitive. Of these two, the power-assertive is often preferred by the child because, once he has been punished, even though it may hurt, you can both forget it. But when you withdraw your love, you are sometimes angry for a long time, so that your child never knows when he has paid for his "crime." The third method, induction, helps your child see *where* he made a mistake or *why* you are angry. It gives your child security to know that you are still loving and that you will teach appropriate behavior.

These three childrearing approaches also influence moral development: when parents employ power-assertive methods, they retard moral development; when they use induction and affection, they increase it (Brophy 1975). By the methods of childrearing that parents use, they become models. Your child accepts guidance only from people he loves and respects.

Preschoolers who are alert and self-controlled have controlling and demanding—but also warm, consistent, and rational—parents who are perceptive to their statements or requests (Baumrind 1967). Parents who fit this description are called "authoritative," *not* "authoritarian." There really is a difference: authoritarian parents are controlling but emotionally unresponsive; authoritative parents show the child love and affection (help the child assume responsibility and independence) while expecting him to meet certain demands and operate within certain controls. Children who have freedom and who have no parental demands do *not* develop maximum curiosity or exhibit exploratory behavior (Brophy 1975).

Dependent, passive, clinging people have been identified as those who were frustrated in infancy, who were rejected and punished severely in the preschool years, and who were in general treated inconsistently. Parents who are overprotective, excessively controlling, and dominating tend to have dependent children (Papalia and Olds 1975).

Children who are highly self-reliant, self-controlled, explorative, and content have parents who are loving, rational, and receptive to the child's communicating, controlling, and demanding. Least self-reliant, most incompetent, and most aimless children are likely to have permissive/indulgent parents who are loving, who encourage independence, and who provide intellectual enrichment, but, while accepting independent behavior, they give the child little *guidance* (Baumrind 1971). When parents treat a child on the child's level of maturity (not as adults or infants), the child tends to be more competent and independent. To help your child build a high regard for himself, you need to be firm in your control, but you need to show respect through your words and actions.

Tactile Stimulation

We learn not only through touching things with our hands, but also through being touched, held, and loved. These experiences aid in physical and emotional development. From the way you touch, your child can tell if you are pleased or displeased: a lot of information is conveyed by a gentle touch or a harsh grip. Bodily contact is one way of reassuring your child that he is valued, has worth, and is loved and accepted.

Guidelines for Parents

If you want to help your child internalize values and other desired characteristics, you (as models) should:

- Give reasons and explain your demands so your child can realize the possible consequences of his actions.
- Set clear and realistic standards for behavior.
- Consistently enforce necessary limits, but give freedom within guidelines.
- Show love and respect as your child questions, protests, or tries to alter situations (Brophy 1975).
- Listen and try to understand so your child can learn about himself and be accepting of new situations and demands.
- Remember that children who habitually avoid new experiences often have a limited view of themselves based on an intellectual inability to see possible actions, a fear of stress or exploring, or a lack of experience.

Self-Image

Introduction

The way your child feels about himself and his sex role (see also the following section) will be very important in his total growth. Feeling like

94

a capable, accepted person and being proud of his sex fills basic needs. As your child gains a conviction of his basic competence, he will grow in self-esteem. There are many ways you can help him in both of these areas.

The single most detrimental factor in a child's self-image is unfair comparisons with other children, which parents often do without thinking. Children don't progress at the same speeds, don't have the same qualities or interest, don't have the same heredity, and certainly they do not have similar experiences. Let's face it: children are all different. Adults who recognize and encourage individual differences help children accept and appreciate individuality. You as parents will have a very strong influence on how your child feels about himself (Baumrind 1972; Coopersmith 1967).

When your child feels strength and power within, he feels self-control. Having something worthwhile to contribute to others is a healthy feeling. When your child is anxious, he feels negative about his body and adequacy. Defensiveness toward self and others is promoted by a negative self-concept. A child who has certain interests may not carry them through because of fear of failure or because of thinking or feeling others would not approve; self desires are inhibited.

Choice Making

Give your child a choice only when he has the opportunity to choose—and when the choice is truly legitimate (for instance, ask, "Do you want an apple or orange?" at snack time, not, "Do you want to go to bed?" when it's bedtime) and when you can accept his decision. When you influence a choice by making one alternative more desirable than the other, you are depriving your child of a valid experience ("Do you want to share or go to your room?"). Of course, the ease or difficulty of choice making is related to your child's age. The average child of three, five, seven, or ten years has an easier time making decisions between two alternatives than do children at other ages (two, four, six, eight, and nine years) because he is under less inner stress and strain at these ages, making choices easier for him to accept without too much emotional conflict. Children do not make good decisions when they are ill, fatigued, bombarded with too many choices, or pressured to conform or overdo (Gesell Institute of Child Development).

Growth and Self-Awareness

In his *Steps to a Healthy Personality* (1950), Erikson points out that, during the fourth and fifth years of life, the child will be working on a "sense of initiative," having ideas and a desire to try them out. He will begin imitating, imagining, questioning, discussing, and trying. His conscience also begins developing. The child needs many activities that will promote initiative, because a failure to develop initiative during these years will result in a "sense of guilt"—a negative and hard-to-lose feeling. Rather than being curious and confident, the child will be overly cautious and unsure of his abilities.

This "sense of initiative" involves more starting than finishing—have you noticed this about *your* child? Your child will plan, undertake, explore, and attack many things; but finishing jobs or doing them well will not be as important now as when he is trying to achieve a "sense of industry" during the sixth through twelfth years.

At no other time in his life will your child be more ready and anxious to learn than he is during the preschool years. He will be eager and able to cooperate with other children in planning and carrying out activities, as well as profiting from experiences with adults.

By age six, basic personality attributes and individual differences are fairly well established (Emmerich 1967). One researcher says even more precisely that fifty percent of the differences between individuals are established "by the age of four for intellectuality in both sexes" (Bloom 1968). Other researchers say it is questionable how much of the child's personality growth will be purposely and voluntarily influenced by his parents (Smart and Smart 1973).

Body Awareness

The term *body image* refers to all the child's responses about his body size, shape, parts, capacities, and environmental interactions (Cratty 1970). If children feel good about their bodies, they also feel good about themselves. Early awareness of body image is shown by the way children draw a person: first the face (mainly the eyes); then the limbs drawn directly from the head. Further awareness involves putting the trunk below the head with heavier limbs attached to it (Cratty 1970). By age three or four the child can understand up and down, as well as front and back, related to his body. Some children at age four and about half of those at age five add details, such as hair, eyes, ears, neck, arms, fingers, legs, and feet, in the proper places. Not until much later (age eight or nine) do most children indicate facial expressions on their drawings (Cratty 1970). This research indicates that children become more aware of their bodies and draw more complete human figures as they increase in age and in the skills necessary to use writing tools.

Guidelines for Parents

If you encourage your child's progress, your relationship will grow; conversely, the more you inhibit your child, the more difficult it will be to communicate with him, and the less he will regard you as a model, and the less definite his self-perception will be. What it all boils down to is this: you are primarily responsible for building self-esteem in your child, and how well you do it will influence his entire life (Hendrick 1975).

It is often easier for an adult to reduce rather than to increase a child's self-esteem. If necessary, write guides and goals to reverse this procedure. Direct your efforts toward the following:

- Motivating good behavior by comparing your child's present actions with his past actions, not by comparing his actions with those of others. Competitiveness and rivalry in children reach a peak around the age of four or five years (Stott and Ball 1957; Hendrick 1975); they compete enough naturally without adults directly encouraging them. Value each child for his individual abilities and assets and play down anything that would make him feel a need to be *best* or *first.*

- Sharing your child's progress toward independence rather than overwhelming and overprotecting him.
- Avoiding negative discussions about your child in his presence. Avoid necessary punishments or discipline when others are around; such an experience can be so humiliating. When you do discipline your child, be firm in your control but explain your child's infraction to him and why you feel your actions are necessary. Such explanation aids your child's growth toward self-esteem (Coopersmith 1967).
- Accepting your child as he is. Appreciate even your child's unsuccessful efforts by giving him *honest* praise and recognition. Eric Erikson (1963) said, "Children cannot be fooled by empty praise and condescending encouragement."

Sex-Role Identification

During recent years, there has been a strong drive to remove the rigid sex-role divisions that have been prevalent for so many years. Physical strength was a requirement for many so-called male roles, so boys were encouraged to be aggressive and self-initiated. Girls were trained to run the home and to develop such characteristics as passivity and dependability. Now members of both sexes are encouraged to choose roles that fit their abilities and interests. To help him understand the many roles that are available, your child needs to have a wide range of experiences. Why limit girls to dolls, cooking, and housekeeping and boys to more muscular tasks like woodworking, block building, and climbing? Girls can benefit from using tools, building, and climbing; boys can benefit from activities formerly classified as *feminine.*

When you look at the materials that are offered for play, try to decide how an *individual* child (regardless of sex) could benefit from playing with them. Children of both sexes need experiences to develop their bodies, minds, and relationships with themselves and others.

Media Influences

Sometimes it is really hard to know what one should or should not do. You can hear, "Boys don't do that," or, "Girls don't act that way," until you are utterly confused. Some examples may be helpful.

In older readers and testing materials, there are many undesirable examples of stereotyped sex roles (Saario, Jacklin, and Tittle 1973). In Newberry prize-winning children's books up to 1969, those about boys outnumber those about girls by three to one (Mitchell 1971); television is even worse. (See "Media and Learning" in Chapter Two for more information.) Is it any wonder that there is confusion about sex roles?

Age and Sex Differences

Usually by two and a half or three years of age a child can categorize human beings as male and female. This is one of the "earliest conceptual classifications made by the child" (Kagan 1971). A little boy once went to see a new baby and was telling his mother about the experience. When asked if the baby was a boy or a girl, he replied: "I don't know. It didn't have its clothes *on*."

Much more research has been done on male than on female sex-role identification. Boys tend to be more physically active and aggressive than girls—perhaps because of the way they are treated. Because boys spend most of their childhood years around adult females (mothers or teachers), their exuberance is often suppressed—even though they need the time, opportunity, and space to release their vigorous energy and especially the chance to see and form a relationship with a male model (Hendrick 1975). A boy's sex-role development is facilitated by the presence of a father (Biller 1969); when the father is absent for long periods of time, especially before the boy is four years old, the boy may take on feminine characteristics. Characteristics of a positive male self-image in boys include the presence of a father, "parental permissiveness, and easy-going attitudes and . . . love-oriented disciplinary techniques" (Spencer 1967).

Aggression is a sex-typed behavior—at least in our culture. Females are usually expected to inhibit physical aggression in all situations; but when seriously threatened, males are expected to fight (Kagan 1971). Numerous studies show that boys exhibit more aggression while girls show more need for affiliation, more interest in people, and more positive feelings toward others (Maccoby 1966). As early as the first year of life males and females show some differences in behavior (see Goldberg and Lewis 1969; Moss 1967).

During the preschool years children tend to imitate and identify with the same-sexed parent more frequently than with the opposite-sexed parent. However, boys seem more clearly aware of their sex roles, since they make masculine choices on preference tests more frequently and consistently than they make feminine choices. Boys show progressively more masculinity each year during the early elementary school grades, but girls tend to reach their femininity peak around five years of age and either maintain or decrease this level during the early elementary school grades (Spencer 1967).

Being able to classify, think, feel, and act in appropriate cultural ways is known as sex typing. Tests and observations of dependency, attachment, and imitation indicate that attitudes toward sex roles change with maturity and are related to mental age (Smart and Smart 1973).

Guidelines for Parents

Simply, the young child needs the following:
- guidelines, or freedom within limits
- a same-sex model, often a parent
- flexibility to try things that complement his interests, needs, and

abilities—regardless of sex
- accurate information about sexual differences
- pride in his sex
- a feeling of being worthwhile as an individual

Anger, Aggression, or Hostility

It is quite a problem for preschoolers to control their emotions. They get angry often because they lack the ability or skills to do something they want, because they get hurt by others, because someone makes them do something they don't want to do, or because they are interrupted. Interruption especially makes children angry. The young child learns things in a chain or sequence of responses (such as rote memorization or steps in a task). When he is interrupted, the child forgets what he is doing, and he has to start all over again. When directed at a goal, the child wants to continue; he then wants to strike out at any individual or object causing an interruption.

Crying, kicking, throwing, biting, and yelling are unproductive expressions of anger during the late infancy and early childhood periods as the child encounters many frustrations in his struggle for independence. Some children handle these frustrations through aggression and hostility, which are other terms for anger.

Modeling

When a person imitates or patterns either appropriate or inappropriate behavior after another (human or animal), it is called *modeling*. One four-year-old was suspected of having a physical problem because of his peculiar walk, but when he was in the presence of his father, who *did* have a physical problem, it was evident why the child walked in such a manner. Another four-year-old with fluent, elaborate language suddenly developed a stutter and a lisp. Carefully checking the child's environment, the parents discovered a new favorite friend who stuttered and lisped. Generally a child imitates the behavior of a person who is loving and caring or who has power and status (Smart and Smart 1973).

Children also model aggressive behavior. When they see live models or when they see human or cartoon models in films, they tend to reproduce the observed behavior in detail. For example, two groups of children viewed films of an adult hitting a large inflated doll (Bandura 1973; Bandura and Huston 1961). In one group, the film showed the adult being rewarded for aggressive behavior; the children in that group imitated the adult. In the second group, the adult was punished for such behavior; the children in that group did *not* imitate the adult. Children in both groups expressed disapproval of the behavior and called the adult "mean, wicked, harsh, and bossy"; but the children still imitated the behavior that was rewarded (either aggressive or non-aggressive behavior). When the second group of children were offered rewards for exhibiting aggressive behavior, they also modeled the aggressive adult.

Do you realize what this means about your relationship to your child? When your child sees you perform aggressive behavior (hitting or yelling) and then sees you profit by it (making someone conform or getting your way), he is going to try the same thing. If you spank your child for hitting someone else—even though you say hitting isn't nice and you extract a promise from him not to do it again—he is learning that hitting (spanking) is a method of control or power. In other words, aggression is a *learned* behavior (Bandura 1973). Although most parents highly dislike children's aggressive behavior, they often exhibit it themselves.

Parental Attitudes

Most parents, although they may believe the stereotype that boys should be able to defend themselves through physical means if necessary, generally prefer verbal over physical forms of aggression (they prefer talking over fighting). Other parents are more permissive and may even encourage their boys to fight. However, most parents discourage children from being aggressive towards them (parents), although they permit aggression on the part of their children against other people. Because of this situation, children soon learn when, how, and to whom they can behave aggressively (Smart and Smart 1973).

Guidelines for Parents

Some steps have been outlined for discouraging physical aggression and encouraging self-control (Goodenough in Smart and Smart 1973). They include the following:
- Meeting the needs of the child (food, rest, and activities) on a flexible schedule but *before* any need becomes critical.
- Giving prompt assistance when the child calls for help.
- Providing many opportunities for the child to make choices within set guidelines.
- Firmly disapproving of aggressive behavior.
- Clearly defining permitted and unpermitted behavior.
- Avoiding physical punishment.
- Forbidding exposure to television programs, films, books, and other media that display aggression and violence.
- Building a loving and accepting emotional atmosphere in the home.

Another way to control your child's anger is to reduce the number of anger-causing frustrations in his life. Being interrupted in the middle of an activity is the number one cause of anger in preschoolers. Try to reduce the number of interruptions for your child by
- Giving your child a few minutes' warning before he must end an activity.
- Making sure your child has large blocks of uninterrupted time.
- Reducing the number of your demands upon your child.

The second source of anger in preschoolers comes from modeling the aggressive behavior of others. Try to control this by
- Selecting models for your child that act appropriately (models can be from books, television, or films, or they can be actual people).

- Discussing ideas about acceptable and nonacceptable behavior.

Another source of aggression and anger for a child is when he can't do things because of a lack of skills or experience or because of limitations placed on him by others. Try

- Providing the activities your child needs for growth, based on his developmental abilities.
- Giving your child opportunities to be successful.

Jealousy

The preschooler will often show jealousy against a family member or an outsider; he will feel frustrated or angry because of the desire to be loved best. Rivalry—wanting to be best or first—may accompany jealousy, or these two feelings may be expressed separately (Smart and Smart 1973). It is the child's self-centered nature to want your full attention and love; if you punish your child for these feelings, he will become even more hostile. Your love and understanding are needed most.

Jealousy Toward Family Members

Jealousy is most apt to occur among siblings. At one time, parents were counseled to prepare their children for a new addition to the family by helping them understand the reproductive process and the features of a new baby; even today, this seems to be good and even helpful. Help your child understand the changes in his mother's body and the changes in your household as you anticipate another family member.

The behavior of a mother toward her children does change during and after pregnancy. She may become short-tempered or impatient as a result of fatigue or illness. Because the changes are associated with pregnancy, the child tends to hold the baby responsible; then, too, the baby is getting many extra privileges such as attention, special food, and the mother's time. Try to give other children privileges, too. Show and tell your child the things he can do to help with the preparations for the baby's arrival. After the baby arrives, include your preschool child in the activities to minimize outbreaks of jealousy.

No matter what type of training you give, your child is going to feel that he is being replaced and that he will be loved less. First children tend to be more jealous and selfish than later children, and in two-child families second children tend to be happier and more generous than first children (Smart and Smart 1973).

But jealousy isn't directed just toward younger siblings. An older brother or sister is bigger, tends to push younger ones around, and can arouse many jealous feelings.

Jealousy Toward Others Outside the Family

As your child expands his social contacts there are more chances of his encountering jealousy. Your child will want peers to play with, but in doing so, he faces the problem of sharing toys, people, and space.

You as parents will have contact with other adults, and if this contact reduces your time with and attention to your child, your child may become resentful.

Guidelines for Parents

Your home should be a place where your child can try his wings in a loving atmosphere; then it will be easier to cope with the many frustrations that will inevitably occur.

Although jealousy and rivalry are inevitable in almost all American families, they can be minimized by

- Preparing your other children for the birth of a new baby, and by reviewing their own infancies.
- Reassuring your children of your love.
- Spending some individual time with each child every day.
- Being understanding, accepting, and aware of your child's emotional feelings while allowing appropriate expression of these feelings.
- Telling each child how important and special he is as an individual.
- Making a strong effort not to compare your children or to arouse competition for affection or privileges.

Fears

What message is your child trying to convey to you when he says:
"I can't go into my room because the Spider Man will get me."
"Penny said she would flush me down the toilet if I didn't let her play with my new doll."
"You can't come to my birthday party if you spank me."
"I'll fall if I climb up there."
"But I *can't* dress myself."
"If I make a mess, Mommy will get mad at me."
These are typical examples of preschoolers' fears. Some of these fears are groundless; some fears, however, actually have value for safety or survival. Fear that is allowed to become generalized, transferred, and unfocused is called anxiety (Smart and Smart 1973); anxiety can be detrimental.

Acquisition of Fears

Fears are very real and threatening, especially to young children, and can be easily acquired in many ways—by conditioning; by scenes viewed on television; by overly demanding social situations; by imagination, initiative, and conscience; by frightening dreams; by experience with animals; by threats to a child's security; and through a number of other sources. A situation or person can produce fear in a child in a single exposure.

The number and kinds of fears a child has are similar to his parents' fears. If parents are afraid of storms, animals, or insects, for instance, they can often pass these fears on to their children through subtle comments ("Don't be afraid") or by actions that let children know their parents are avoiding something unpleasant. Overprotective parents convey feelings of danger and fear through both attitudes and behavior (Papalia and Olds 1975).

When four- and five-year-olds were interviewed, they revealed fear derived from watching violent cartoon and human characters on television. Their recollection a week following their viewing of (1) nonviolent shows, (2) violent shows with human actors, and (3) violent cartoons was brighter concerning the human violence film than the other two types (Osborn and Endsley 1971).

Growth and Fears

During the fourth and fifth years—because of the increase in imagination, initiative, and conscience (Erikson 1950)—children sometimes go beyond set limits. The developing conscience may tell them that they are doing or that they want to do wrong, so they may create imaginative situations—many of which are frightening. They may imagine powerful animals with aggressive characteristics they'd like to have.

Reporting on the dreams of their children between birth and six years of age, parents indicated a progressive decrease in fears of tangible stimuli (such as objects, noises, falls, and strange people), and an increase in fears of intangible stimuli (such as imaginary creatures, darkness, aloneness, abandonment, and threat or danger of bodily injury and harm) (Jersild and Holmes 1935).

When 130 children five years or older were questioned about their fears, animals were mentioned most often, but less so as the age of the children increased (eighty percent of five- and six-year-olds were afraid of animals, but only seventy-three percent of seven- and eight-year-olds had that fear). Snakes ranked number one on the fear list—with the lion, tiger, and bear following. It is interesting to note that the fears parents *try* to teach (such as traffic hazards, germs, and kidnappers) were rarely cited by the children (Maurer 1965).

Fear of Separation

Recently a study was conducted to determine how anxious two-year-olds became when they were separated from their parents. One group of children attended a nursery during the day and returned home at night, while another group (residential nursery attenders) lived in a nursery twenty-four hours a day because of special home conditions. After no behavioral differences during the first two days, the residential children anxiously sought more adult attention and affection; they regressed to more crying, thumb and finger sucking, and more toilet accidents; they had more illnesses (colds); and they exhibited more and greater hostility. The conclusion was that *complete* separation from the parents is likely to be destructive, but that partial separation is not necessarily so (Smart and Smart 1973).

Separation (through divorce, death, or some other reason), if interpreted by the young child as due to his own unworthiness, could cause

103

a separation anxiety. Fathers are more likely than mothers to cause this anxiety in preschool children because they more frequently leave the households (Smart and Smart 1973).

Separation anxiety relates to the topic of working mothers. Although there is a general feeling that mothers of young children should be at home with their children rather than in the working force, a thorough review of research on maternal employment concludes that it is "too global a condition to use as a variable in investigating causes of children's behavior" (Stoltz 1960). When twenty-six kindergarten children were matched for working and nonworking mothers, no differences were found on nine personality characteristics (Siegel, et al. 1959). Other factors are more important to separation anxiety than whether or not a mother works outside the home: they include her acceptance of her role, "the quality of substitute care provided, the age and sex of the child, the relation of the mother's employment to family functioning and its meaning to husband-wife relations" (Stoltz 1960).

Guidelines for Parents

Since fear is not a pleasant feeling, you probably want to minimize it in your child. The best way is to involve your child in gradually increasing contacts with things that are frightening. *Forcing* your child to deal with a fearful situation will only intensify his fear. Success and competence will come when your child learns to deal with his own fears—but your help will be needed. Explaining a situation or belittling your child because of his fear is *not* helpful. These fears are real to him, and until your child can have some reassuring experiences, the fears will remain. When your child expresses fear, he needs immediate understanding and acceptance of the feeling. Show your love and understanding.

Although it is inevitable that young children will have some fears, the way children and parents react to them will result in their dissolution or magnification. Most children need some external help in accepting and dealing with their fears. Here are some aids that you could apply:

- When there is to be a parent-child separation, make a gradual transition:
  - Take your child to his grandma's house or to the babysitter's for a short visit first.
  - Let your child stay with a loved one during a crisis (your child can handle separation from you better if he is with a loved person).
  - Acquaint your child with a friendly adult and leave him for very short periods of time after reassurance of your return. (If you often sneak out when your child least expects it, he will become *more* fearful of a separation and will trust you less.)
- When your child displays a spontaneous expression of fear, try to understand your child's feelings and help him develop ways for dealing with them.
- When you are aware of upcoming situations that will be fearful for

your child (hospitalization, for example), help your child understand by providing stories, conversations, and dramatic play.

- Make frightening situations less threatening—and never force your child into a feared situation:
  - If your child is afraid to gather eggs, shoo the chickens out of the henhouse before asking your child to go in. Those hens are so noisy and have such sharp beaks; they really are frightening.
  - If your child fears a big barking dog that you *know* is harmless, tie it up and let your child approach it gradually. It may take several attempts for your child even to get close, but progress is what counts.
  - If your child is afraid to go to bed at night, leave a light on or let him have a flashlight to focus on things that seem scary.
  - If your child awakens from a bad dream, help him see that it was not real. Be comforting and leave a light on (if necessary), but put the child back into his own bed.
  - If your child is afraid of animals, get a small pet that he can care for as it grows up.
  - If your child is afraid of other children, invite them to your house (a familiar and safe place) to play.

Creative Expression

"Sense of Initiative"

Corresponding with Erikson's *"sense of initiative,"* the four- to six-year-old is reaching out, exploring, discovering, and showing curiosity. This is a peak period of creativity and self-expression (Hendrick 1975); with materials that can be used in many ways (such as fingerpaint, collage, cutting and pasting, and clay), the child feels free to express creative and emotional ideas and feelings. He can't fail, because there is no standard to reach.

It is healthy for children to learn to handle their feelings. They become aware of their bodies and movements, but most of all they can express their emotional feelings as they exhibit individuality, increase self-image, and explore the world. If children can satisfactorily solve their problems while they have imagination and initiative, they will use the same techniques to "enliven, sparkle, inspire, and push throughout the rest of life" because "both creativity and true recreation have their roots in imaginative play" (Smart and Smart 1972).

All children pass through general stages of development in using creative artistic materials. First of all, curiosity prompts them to explore and manipulate. After gaining some skills, their next move is to the *non-representational* stage; *nonrepresentational* pictures have design and intention that are recognizable only to the painter. In fact, a child in this stage may change his mind many times about what he is painting as it takes form or as it reminds the child of something. (Don't ask, "What are you making?" because your child probably doesn't know, either. Rather, say, "Tell me about your picture.") The next stage is called *representational;* now a deliberate goal is set, and the picture is generally recognizable by people other than the artist. Some children reach this stage earlier, but most develop it during the fifth, or kindergarten, year (Hendricks 1975). From one to three years of age, the child scribbles (*a very important part* of creative development); from two to five years of age, shape and design appear in the child's work; from age four onward is the pictorial stage (Smart and Smart 1973).

You can help your child explore and understand the world if you will provide countless opportunities for him to use a variety of materials with limitless possibilities and without expecting him to end up with a specific product. Sometimes your child *will* make a product, but that is unimportant now. Various materials and how they're used, the time that is provided, and the motivation will stimulate participation and enjoyment of such activities.

Coloring books have no use or value at this stage of development; in fact, they have been known to stifle, not stimulate, creativity. They are too restricting and perfect for the preschooler's limited muscle and eye skills. The child needs to scribble (large-muscle movements) and set up his own evaluative scale (how and what to draw). Firsthand experiences will give him ideas, and constructive experiences will give him confidence and skills.

Art experiences with emphasis on the process of creating, not on following established patterns, will help your child develop

- self-image (originality, independence, confidence, and self-acceptance)
- clearer ideas and concepts
- muscle and eye skills
- social and emotional techniques
- self-expression and aesthetic appreciation
- constructive release of feelings

"Play is a Child's Work"

Play is another important part of creativity. Whatever comes to mind can be expressed in play: there is no right or wrong way to react to play situations, and the ideas may be short-lived or can be used over a long period of time. Play is serious business for the preschool child, and it is essential for his healthy development (Curry and Arnaud 1971; Frank 1968; Millar 1968). During the last decade, when there has been such a strong emphasis on intellectual development, many adults (teachers and parents) have tended to underestimate or exclude play. Despite their efforts, play always has and always will occupy a place of importance in children's lives. Play in and of itself is refreshing and spontaneous; while it gives the appearance of frivolity and aimlessness, it provides experiences the child needs for growing and for understanding the world. Those who look at play as a mere time-consumer have lost their youth, vitality, and true perspective of what time really means.

106

Play fulfills many purposes:

- It enhances and advances *physical development* (Hartley, Frank, and Goldenson 1952).
- It stimulates *intellectual development* by providing one of the best ways to exercise symbolic (abstract) thought. The child tries out ideas or experiences, lays the foundation for more learning, and clarifies his firsthand experiences (Piaget 1962).
- It promotes *social development.* One of the earliest forms of play is solitary—the child plays alone. Then the child plays beside, but not with, another child (parallel play). Later he can interact verbally and cooperatively with one or more people in imitative, make-believe, or original situations for sustained periods of time. Play helps the child understand the important aspects of interacting with others as well as how to put himself in another's place (Smilansky 1968; El'Konin 1969; Kohlberg 1969). The child grows in empathy and consideration, learning some of the social rules of getting along with others.
- It gives an expression to and relief of positive and negative feelings, thus developing *emotional* values (Axline 1969) and helping the child master his environment.
- Then there are *creative* benefits. Children playing can be in control and try their very own ideas, or they can modify events that they have seen. If they don't like a situation, they can change it. They can issue commands or sit back and let others make demands. There is no standard to reach, so they can relax and enjoy the experience. There are strong indications that playfulness and divergent thinking are related to each other, but which comes first has not been established (Lieberman 1968).

Organized games are less appropriate for young children than for older ones, because games require a level of performance, are based on skills that are not yet developed, and require stereotyped behavior. Leave games for later years, when conformity will be important to your child.

You can help your child enter into and enjoy creative play by taking a passive role and by letting him dominate the activity. You can help by offering occasional play techniques, by encouraging your child to initiate and use his ideas, and by providing a rich background of experiences as he is ready.

When you buy toys and equipment, be sure to get things that are limited only by your child's imagination. Things that can be used only in certain ways—wind-up toys or some manipulative toys, for instance—are not generally the best for preschool children. Get things your child can use in lots of ways—blocks, wooden and rubber figures, clay, and so on. Interacting with a friend or peer also adds enjoyment and stimulation for your child.

Young preschool children (mainly three-year-olds) generally portray scenes of home and of their familiar environment when they play. By the end of the preschool years (ages four and a half or five) children who have been unlimited in their experiences employ for sociodramatic play a wide range of topics—many of which they have heard about or have seen on television but have not personally experienced. Observe your child's dramatic play, and you will see the appropriateness of imagination in dealing with reality. Pretending helps your child cope with his problems, because frustrating experiences can be eliminated or changed. Your preschooler will probably also maintain new ideas and be willing to experiment with them because his ideas and expressions will be fluid and valued.

Your child's dramatic play may surprise (or embarrass) you when he repeats your behavior. Situations, activities, and words you thought went unnoticed (or that you wish had never happened) may now be staged before you in detail. This is because your child portrays roles of people who are important to him, and you rank very high. He will imitate your behavior (mannerisms, sayings, and so on), your thinking, your standards, and your goals—whether they are good or bad. Your child is unable to select out and follow just the good things you do and to forget the others.

Imagination—*not* fantasy—is the key to personality development during the late preschool years. Imagination originates within your child's own mind, while fantasy is something that is generally imposed from outside (through stories, movies, or television, for instance). Your child can handle imagination; fantasy often controls him now, but will play an important part in the following years. Through imagination your child can invent props if they are not provided (for example, a block could become a gun, a baby, or a car). Your child may have his own private jargon or meanings while expressing roles, relationships, or language in an effort to reduce anxiety or show individuality.

Imaginary Companions

Imaginary companions are quite common during the preschool years: a fourth to a third of all children have them (Smart and Smart 1973). They come at a time when your child is developing initiative—together with its component, imagination—so it should be no surprise if imaginary companions come
- in the form of animals or humans
- individually or in groups
- only for a short time or for a long duration
- as ideals or scapegoats
- more often to bright children and to girls

Guidelines for Parents

Providing opportunities for creative expression through art, music, language, and dramatic play will be one of the most important things you can do to further your child's development in all areas (physical, intellectual, social, emotional, and spiritual). Your positive attitude toward these creative experiences will be stimulating and motivating for him.

There are some important ways that you can encourage participation in creative experiences:

- Provide your child with a wide variety of materials and opportunities.
- Don't interfere with your child's project unless he asks or he really needs you.
- Let your child do his own thing without forcing him to follow your example or direction.
- Since the *process* is far more important than the *product,* let your child work on his own.
- See that your child has lots of time and opportunity to work.
- Compliment your child on his initiative and enjoyment rather than passing judgment on his creation (Sparling and Sparling 1973).
- Grant your child the right to refuse or withdraw from a situation.
- See that your child has materials to enjoy—and make sure the materials feature quantity, variety, and beauty.

Activities for Creative Expression

Because many activities that could be included here are already discussed in various sections of this book, only a few basic suggestions and recipes for some art activities will be included here. By excluding a list here, the reader is reminded that opportunities for creative self-expression are vital to the child's *total growth* and that they should be carefully and frequently provided.

Art

Provide open-ended activities where no set standard or product is expected, and let your child explore and experiment. Such activities include fingerpainting, modeling clay, making collages, painting, stringing, woodworking, playing with building blocks, and so on. (For extensive discussion and lists of activities, see Taylor 1974; 1975, pp. 31–77.)

Recipes

Involve your child in making, using, and cleaning up activities.

Fingerpaint (A squirt of liquid detergent aids in cleanup)

Method 1: Mix equal amounts of soap flakes and powdered laundry starch with enough water to make the paint the consistency of whipped potatoes. Add coloring if desired; food coloring may stain your child's hands and some surfaces; powdered paint is better to use.

Method 2: With an egg or electric beater, whip soap *flakes* and a small amount of water to the desired consistency.

Method 3: Dissolve ¼ cup of cornstarch in cold water. Add 4 cups of boiling water; bring the mixture to a boil. Add color. For different textures add sand, oatmeal, sugar, glycerine, cornstarch, or flour.

Method 4: Stir 1 cup of flour and 1½ cups of salt into ¾ cups of water. Add coloring. (This method produces paint with a grainy quality.)

Method 5: Put the desired amount of water into a pan. Sprinkle wallpaper flour on top of the water, a small amount at a time. Stir the mixture in a circular motion until all the lumps are gone. Add more wallpaper flour until the paint reaches a desired consistency (it should be similar to liquid laundry starch).

Method 6: Pour liquid starch on a wet surface. Add color if desired.

The following products could be used, but should be used *cautiously* because of cost, waste, and difficulty in cleanup: salt-flour-water mixture, toothpaste, mashed potatoes, buttermilk, cooked oatmeal, pudding, cold cream, shaving cream, chocolate syrup, or solid and liquid shortening.

Clay

Flour-Salt Dough: Mix 2 cups of flour with 1 cup of salt. Add a small amount of liquid oil to keep the dough from drying out and enough water to work the mixture into a pliable dough. Food coloring can be added to the water, or powdered paint can be added to the dry ingredients. The mixture should be the consistency of cookie dough.

Cornstarch Dough: Mix 2 cups of salt and ⅔ cup of water in a pan, and bring the mixture to a boil. Stir 1 cup of cornstarch and ⅔ cup of water together; add to the salt water mixture, and knead well. Store the mixture in a covered container in the refrigerator.

Cooked Clay: Blend ½ of a cup of cornstarch with a small amount of cold water. Boil 4 cups of water, add 1 cup of salt, and then add this mixture to the cornstarch mixture and cook it in a double boiler until it is clear. Cool the mixture overnight. Knead 1 cup of flour into the mixture until it is the right consistency (coloring may be added with the flour). Keep the dough in an airtight container; if it becomes hard, add more water as needed.

Bread Dough Art: Mix 4 cups of flour, 1 cup of salt, and 1⅔ cups of water. Knead the bread dough until it is a working consistency, but don't let it dry out; bake it within 2 to 3 hours at 275 degrees for 3½ to 4 hours. Paint the dough with acrylic paint, and finish it with resin spray for protection. (As an alternative to the resin, brush the dough with egg white before baking.)

Collages

A collage is a conglomerate of things arranged to the originator's desire and adhered to a background. A few things found at home that could be used to make a collage are: *building materials* such as bark, sand, screen, shavings, wood, and wire; *food products,* especially dried staples like rice or beans, egg shells, macaroni, seeds, and popcorn; *fabrics* such as burlap, corduroy, fur, and knits; *sewing notions* such as beads, buttons, spools, ribbon, string, and yarn; *paper and paper substitutes* such as foil, blotters, boxes, cardboard, greeting cards, magazines, stamps, straws, and wallpaper; and *mis-*

cellaneous items such as bottle caps, corks, feathers, flowers, leaves, pipe cleaners, shells, and toothpicks. (For more details, see Taylor, 1975, pp. 45–47.)

Painting

Many different kinds of painting can be provided: easel, sponge, block, straw, spool, string, towel, dry, bubble, doily, and many more. (For details see Taylor, 1975, pp. 52-59.)

Stringing

This may be somewhat tedious for preschool children, but opportunities should be provided to string such items as large beads, breakfast cereals, colored straws cut in one-half inch lengths, cranberries, fabrics, rigatoni, paper, or spools.

"Strings" for threading could be shoelaces or yarn or string with the ends stiffened by wax, scotch tape, or starch. A large needle could be provided for older children.

Fruit Leather

Select ripe fruit for maximum flavor. Suggested fruits are apples, apricots, peaches, pears, plums, raspberries, and rhubarb. Wash and puree the fruit in a blender; add sweetening and flavoring if they are desired. Line a cookie sheet with plastic wrap, and spread the puree approximately ¼-inch thick evenly over the plastic. One 17-inch by 12-inch cookie sheet will hold about two or three cups of puree. For easy removal, leave the plastic a bit larger than the cookie sheet. Dry the puree in direct sunlight for nine to ten hours in either a screened box, a home dryer, or covered with gauze. The fruit leather is ready when it is leathery and chewy. While the fruit is still warm, roll it jellyroll fashion, removing the plastic. The fruit leather can be stored in glass jars or in plastic bags.

Music

Your child should have experience with many kinds of music—some for participation and some for listening enjoyment. Be sure to include excursions to local and cultural music events. (For a discussion and suggestions concerning music, see Taylor, 1975, pp. 93–106.)

Dramatic Play

This is important for your child's knowledge about people and his environment. Take your child to the places where ideas are available; then provide time, space, props, and opportunities for your child's involvement. (For a discussion and suggestions, see Taylor, 1975, pp. 49–52.)

Language

Language has been discussed throughout this book in general and in Chapter Two in more detail; for further discussion and activities, see Taylor, 1975, pp. 77–92.

References for Emotional Development:

Baumrind, D., "Current Patterns of Parental Authority," *Developmental Psychology Monographs,* 4:1971, 1, Part 2.

Baumrind, D., "Child Care Practices Anteceding Three Patterns of Preschool Behavior," *Genetic Psychology Monographs, 75,* 1967, 43–88.

Brophy, Jere E., Thomas L. Good, and Shari E. Nedler, *Teaching in the Preschool,* New York: Harper and Row Publishers, 1975.

Carson, R., *The Sense of Wonder,* New York: Harper and Row Publishers, 1956.

Coopersmith, S., *The Antecedents of Self-Esteem,* San Francisco: Freeman, 1967.

DiBartolo, R., and W. E. Vinacke, "Adult Nurturance and the Preschool Child," *Developmental Psychology, 1,* 1969, 247–251.

Epstein, S., "The Self-Concept Revisited: Or a Theory of a Theory," *American Psychologist,* 28 (1973), 404–416.

Erikson, Eric, *Childhood and Society,* 2nd ed., New York: Norton, 1963.

Erikson, Eric, *A Healthy Personality for Your Child,* Washington, D.C.: Supt. of Documents, Result of Midcentury White House Conference on Children and Youth, December 1950.

Hendrick, Joanne, *The Whole Child: New Trends in Early Education,* St. Louis: The C. V. Mosby Company, 1975.

Hoffman, M., "Moral Development," in P. Mussen, ed., *Carmichael's Manual of Child Psychology,* 3rd ed., vol. 2, New York: Wiley, 1970.

Lillie, David L., *Early Childhood Education,* Chicago: Science Research Associates, Inc., 1975.

Lorenz, K., "The Enmity Between Generations and Its Probable Ethological Causes," in M. Piers, ed., *Play and Development,* New York: Norton, 1972.

Medinnus, G., and F. Curtis, "The Relation between Maternal Self-Acceptance and Child Acceptance," *Journal of Consulting Psychology,* 27 (1963), 542–544.

Papalia, Diane E., and Sally W. Olds, *A Child's World,* New York: McGraw-Hill Book Company, 1975.

Sigel, I. E., R. Starr, A. Secrist, J. P. Jackson, and E. Hill, "Social and Emotional Development of Young Children," in J. L. Frost, ed., *Revisiting Early Childhood Education: Readings,* New York: Holt, Rinehart and Winston, 1973.

Smart, Mollie, and Russell C. Smart, *Preschool Children: Development and Relationships,* New York: Macmillan, 1973.

White, Burton, "Fundamental Early Environmental Influences on the Development of Competence," in M. Meyer, ed., *Third Symposium on Learning: Cognitive Learning,* Bellingham, Wash.: Western Washington State College, 1972.

Wood, Mary M., *The Rutland Center Model for Treating Emotionally Disturbed Children,* Athens, Georgia: Rutland Center Technical Assistance Office, 1972.

References for Self-Image and Sex Role Identification:

Baumrind, D., "Socialization and Instrumental Competence in Young Children," in W. W. Hartup, ed., *The Young Child: Review of Research,* vol. 2, Washington, D.C.: NAEYC, 1972.

Biber, Barbara, *Premature Structuring As a Deterrent to Creativity,* New York: Bank Street College of Education, Publication #67.

Biller, H. B., "Father Absence, Maternal Encouragement and Sex Role Development in Kindergarten-age Boys," *Child Development, 40,* 1969, 539–546.

Block, J., "Conceptions of Sex Role: Some Crosscultural and Longitudinal Perspectives," *American Psychologist,* 28 (1973), 512–526.

Bloom, B., *Stability and Change in Human Characteristics,* New York: Wiley, 1964.

Briggs, D. C., *Your Child's Self-Esteem. The Key to His Life,* Garden City, N.Y.: Doubleday and Company, Inc., 1970.

Brophy, Jere E., Thomas L. Good, and Shari E. Nedler, *Teaching in the Preschool,* New York: Harper and Row Publishers, 1975.

Coopersmith, S., *The Antecedents of Self-Esteem,* San Francisco, Calif.: Freeman, 1967.

Cratty, B. J., *Perceptual and Motor Development in Infants and Children,* New York: Macmillan, 1970.

Emmerich, Walter, "Stability and Change in Early Personality Development," in Hartup, W. W. and N. L. Smothergill, eds., *The Young Child: Review of Research,* vol. I, Washington, D.C.: NAEYC, 1967, pp. 248–261.

Erickson, Eric, *A Healthy Personality for Your Child,* Washington, D.C.: Supt. of Documents, December 1950.

Erikson, Eric, *Childhood and Society,* 2nd ed., New York: Norton, 1963.

Goldberg, S., and M. Lewis, "Play Behavior in the Year-Old Infant: Early Sex Differences," *Child Development,* 40, 1969, 21–31.

Hendrick, Joanne, *The Whole Child: New Trends in Early Education,* St. Louis: The C. V. Mosby Company, 1975.

Kagan, Jerome, *Understanding Children: Behavior, Motives, and Thought,* New York: Harcourt Brace Jovanovich, Inc., 1971.

Kirkhart, R., and E. Kirkhart, "The Bruised Self: Mending in the Early Years," in K. Yamamoto, ed., *The Child and His Image: Self-Concept in the Early Years,* Boston: Houghton Mifflin Company, 1972.

Maccoby, E. E., ed., *The Development of Sex Differences,* Stanford, Calif.: Stanford University Press, 1966.

Mitchell, E., "The Learning of Sex Roles Through Toys and Books," *Young Children,* 28, 1971, (4), 226–232.

Moss, H., "Sex, Age and State as Determinants of Mother-Infant Interaction," *Merrill-Palmer Quarterly,* 13, 1967, (1), 19–36.

Mussen, P. H., J. J. Conger, and J. Kagan, *Child Development and Personality,* New York: Harper and Row Publishers, 1969.

Papalia, Diane E., and Sally W. Olds, *A Child's World,* New York: McGraw-Hill Book Company, 1975.

Ruebush, B. K., *Children's Behavior as a Function of Anxiety and Defensiveness,* Unpublished Doctoral Dissertation, Yale University, 1960.

Saario, T., C. N. Jacklin, and C. K. Tittle, "Sex Role Stereotyping in the Public Schools," *Harvard Educational Review,* 43 (3), 1973, 386–416.

Smart, Mollie, and Russell C. Smart, *Preschool Children: Development and Relationships,* New York: Macmillan, 1973.

Spencer, T. D., "Sex-Role Learning in Early Childhood," in W. W. Hartup and N. L. Smothergill, eds., *The Young Child: Review of Research,* vol. I, Washington, D.C.: NAFYC, 1967, pp. 193–205.

Stott, L. H., and R. S. Ball, "Consistency and Change in Ascendance-Submission in the Social Interaction of Children," *Child Development,* 28, 1957, 259–272.

References for Dealing with Anger, Aggression, and Hostility:

Bandura, A., *Aggression: A Social Learning Analysis,* Englewood Cliffs, N.J.:

Prentice-Hall, Inc., 1973.

Bandura, A., and A. H. Huston, "Identification as a Process of Incidental Learning," *Journal of Abnormal Social Psychology, 63,* 1961, 311–318.

Kagan, Jerome, *Understanding Children: Behavior, Motives, and Thought,* New York: Harcourt Brace Jovanovich, Inc., 1971.

Smart, Mollie, and Russell C. Smart, *Preschool Children: Development and Relationships,* New York: Macmillan, 1973.

References for Dealing with Jealousy:

Smart, Mollie, and Russell C. Smart, *Preschool Children: Development and Relationships,* New York: Macmillan, 1973.

References for Dealing with Fears:

Erikson, Eric, *A Healthy Personality for Your Child,* Washington, D.C.: Supt. of Documents, December, 1950.

Jersild, A. T. and Holmes, F. B., "Children's Fears," *Child Development Monographs,* no. 20, New York: Teachers College, Columbia University, 1935.

Maurer, A., "What Children Fear," *Journal of Genetic Psychology, 106,* 1965, 265–277.

Osborn, D. K., and R. C. Endsley, "Emotional Reactions of Young Children to TV Violence," *Child Development, 42,* 1971, 321–333.

Papalia, Diane E., and Sally W. Olds, *A Child's World,* New York: McGraw-Hill, 1975.

Siegel, A. E., L. M. Stoltz, E. A. Hitchcock, and J. M. Adamson, "Dependence and Independence in the Children of Working Mothers," *Child Development, 30,* 1959, 533–546.

Smart, Mollie, and Russell C. Smart, *Preschool Children: Development and Relationships,* New York: Macmillan, 1973.

Stoltz, L. M., "Effects of Maternal Employment on Children: Evidence from Research," *Child Development,* 31, 1960, 749–782.

References for Creative Expression:

Axline, V. M., *Play Therapy,* rev. ed., New York: Ballantine Books, Inc., 1969.

Biber, Barbara, *Premature Structuring As a Deterrent to Creativity,* New York: Bank Street College of Education, Publication #67.

Curry, N. E., and S. Arnaud, eds., *Play: the Child Strives Toward Self-Realization,* Washington, D.C.: NAEYC, 1971.

El'Konin, D. B., "Some Results of the Study of the Psychological Development of Preschool-age Children," in M. Cole and I. Maltzman, eds., *A Handbook of Contemporary Soviet Psychology,* New York: Basic Books, Inc., Publishers, 1969.

Frank, L. K., "Play Is Valid," *Childhood Education,* 44, 1968, 433–440.

Griffiths, Ruth, *A Study of Imagination in Early Childhood,* London: Kegan, Paul, Trench, Trubner, 1935.

Hartley, R. E., L. K. Frank, and R. M. Goldenson, *Understanding Children's Play,* New York: Columbia University Press, 1952.

Hendrick, Joanne, *The Whole Child: New Trends in Early Education,* St. Louis: The C. V. Mosby Company, 1975.

Kellogg, R., and S. O'Dell, *Analyzing Children's Art,* Palo Alto, Calif.: National Press Books, 1969.

Kohlberg, L., "Stage and Sequence: The Cognitive-Developmental Approach to Socialization," in D. A. Goslin, ed., *Handbook of Socialization and Research,* Chicago: Rand McNally and Company, 1969.

Lieberman, J. N., "Playfulness and Divergent Thinking Ability: an Investigation of Their Relationship at the Kindergarten Level," in M. Almy, ed., *Early Childhood Play: Selected Readings Related to Cognition and Motivation,* New York: Simon and Schuster, Inc., 1968.

Lowenfeld, V., *Your Child and His Art: A Guide for Parents,* New York: Macmillan, 1954.

Marzollo, J., and J. Lloyd, *Learning Through Play,* New York: Harper and Row, 1972.

Matterson, E. M., *Play and Playthings for the Preschool Child,* Baltimore, Md.: Penguin Books, Inc., 1965.

Maynard, F., *Guiding Your Child to a More Creative Life,* Garden City, N.Y.: Doubleday and Company, 1973.

Millar, S., *The Psychology of Play,* Baltimore, Md.: Penguin Books, Inc., 1968.

Piaget, J., *Play, Dreams, and Imitation in Childhood,* New York: W. W. Norton and Company, Inc., 1962.

Pitcher, E. G., and Prelinger, E., *Children Tell Stories: An Analysis of Fantasy,* New York: International Universities Press, 1963.

Smart, Mollie, and Russell C. Smart, *Preschool Children: Development and Relationships,* New York: Macmillan, 1973.

Smart, M. S., and R. C. Smart, *Child Development and Relationships,* 2nd ed., New York: Macmillan, 1972.

Smilansky, S., *The Effects of Sociodramatic Play on Disadvantaged Children,* New York: John Wiley and Sons, Inc., 1968.

Sparling, J. J., and M. C. Sparling, "How to Talk to a Scribbler," *Young Children,* 28 (6), 1973, 333–341.

Sutton-Smith, Brian, "The Role of Play in Cognitive Development," in Hartup, W. W. and N. L. Smothergill, eds., *The Young Child: Review of Research,* vol. I, Washington, D.C.: NAEYC, 1967, pp. 96–108. Also in *Young Children,* 1967, 22, 361–370.

Sutton-Smith, B., "A Syntax for Play and Games," in R. E. Herron and B. Sutton-Smith, eds., *Child's Play,* New York: John Wiley and Sons, Inc., 1971.

Taylor, Barbara J., *A Child Goes Forth,* rev. ed., Provo, Utah: Brigham Young University Press, 1975.

Taylor, Barbara J., *When I Do, I Learn,* Provo, Utah: Brigham Young University Press, 1974.

Torrance, E. P., *Creativity,* Belmont, Calif.: Fearon Publishers, 1969.

Torrance, E. Paul, *Guiding Creative Talent,* Englewood Cliffs, N.J.: Prentice-Hall, Inc., 1962.

Four

Social Development

A Note from Your Preschooler

Dear Mom and Dad,

I need to learn how to talk and do other things better so I can have more fun playing with my friends. I have to feel safe at home and other places and I need to know who I am and what I can do. Sometimes I need to say, "No!" But I also have to learn to share things and people, and take turns. I want to be friends with kids my age and with other people, too.

Sometimes I make lots of mistakes. When I get an idea, I *have* to do it *right now.* Please understand—love me, help me, and wait for me. When I do something wrong, I learn to do better next time.

I can only see things *my* way. I want everything I see—for as long as I want it. I can't understand when someone else feels bad unless I am sad or mad, too.

Since I don't have a lot of words in my head or my mouth yet, I watch and listen to others. Because I am around you most, I do and say things like you. I also copy other people I know and even people on TV. What I see is what I do, so please be careful what you let me see.

I'm big enough to help you make the rules for what I can and can't do. That way I'll be good more often—but you still have to explain things to me and understand when I'm bad.

Sometimes you want me to do things I just *can't* do—like play nice with company. When I yell at you in the store, kick the benches in church, or fight with my little brother, I'm really not trying to be bad. But sometimes you want me to act bigger than I am. Other times you don't even explain what you want me to do. Once in a while I'm bad on purpose—please don't let me do this.

We can have lots of good times and fun talks together—if you use your ears and eyes to learn what I *really* want or need.

      Love,
      Your Preschooler

Introduction

Social development involves caring about self and about relationships—whether they are positive or negative—with other individuals and groups. Through physical activities such as running, tasting, and playing, a child first learns to trust his own body. Then he learns to satisfy his needs through verbal communication—by naming objects, by following simple instructions, and by speaking spontaneous words and sentences. The child gradually becomes more social, using verbal and nonverbal contacts as he learns to trust others. Further progress develops some preacademic skills, such as understanding and using language; coloring, cutting, and pasting; listening and responding to simple stories; and coordinating eyes and hands for dressing and drawing. These skills are necessary for thinking, for language development, and for body coordination (Wood 1972).

You are your child's most trusted and valued teacher; you can help him learn to accept himself and others. Patiently help your child learn to cope with the world: teach him how to develop realistic expectations, limitations, and performances and how to develop cooperation and respect for individual differences among his peers.

Societal Interaction

Behavioral Changes

You will recall that, during the toddler and early preschool years, your child was striving hard to develop autonomy, but during the late preschool years he is striving just as hard to develop a "sense of initiative." Although you may become frustrated with his curiosity, his desire to seek new experiences, or his desire to try all sorts of things, your child's questions and interest will be endless—questions help your child understand past experiences and integrate them into a more complex environment.

If your child's attempts to do things are successful and satisfying, your child will find his abilities and confidence greatly increased. He will continue to become involved in new ideas, in questions and answers, in better methods of problem solving, in reasoning, and in creativity.

You may feel that you are losing control of your child because he is becoming more and more independent; you may even feel uncomfortable and threatened by his desire and struggle for independence. Remember that this is a part of growing up for *both* of you. Your child may begin to be more self-assertive; this is similar to aggression, but it does not imply anger—assertiveness only indicates his ability to interact with and control his environment.

As his conscience begins to develop, it will attempt to regulate your child's initiative and imagination. He will seek clues from you in determining what is right and wrong, but sometimes initiative and imagination will try to overrule conscience and your child may have guilt feelings over this conflict; however, "the establishment of a healthy sense of initiative means that a child can interact vigorously under the control

118

of a conscience that is strong enough but not too punishing" (Smart and Smart 1973).

Socialization

Your child may express feelings of dependency or attachment—feelings that are similar but that are not identical. Attachment is an affectionate tie to a particular *person;* dependency involves wanting some *thing*—such as assistance, attention, approval, recognition, contact, or closeness—and not the person who gives it (Smart and Smart 1973). Because your child may feel that only you or some other specific person can assist or accompany him, provide experiences that will help teach him the fact that many people (such as teachers, neighbors, and other adults outside the home) are accepting and trustworthy. Dependence can be reduced as your child builds confidence in himself in dealing with his environment.

When your child is three or four years of age, you will notice (with relief!) the appearance of cooperative behavior. As your child imitates the behavior of others and seeks approval or reassurance, he will be more cooperative because of his better understanding of language, social techniques, and experiences.

The three- and four-year-old will like to play with children in:
- same-sex groups of two
- unstructured competition
- leadership roles (in the form of bully or diplomat)

Between five and six years of age children want:
- three or more playing together using simple rules
- cooperative behavior
- simple leadership patterns
- social stimuli—influence of peers or culture (Cratty 1970)

As your child grows older, quarrels between him and other children will decrease in number but will increase in length (Dawe 1934). Although your child settled differences rather quickly at a young age, he will tend to extend them longer as his social contacts increase (Maudry and Nekula 1939). Feelings of rivalry and competition reach a peak between the ages of four and six (Greenberg 1932), but the intensity of these feelings may vary with individual children.

Generosity may appear during the preschool years; it is more prevalent with increased age (Hartup and Coates 1967) and with modeling—when your child sees you being generous, for instance (Hendrick 1975). The ability for your child to put himself in another's place through role playing also encourages his generosity (Flavell 1966).

Almost all children under the age of seven are primarily egocentric; they see things only from their own points of view—everything is "I" or "me" (Piaget 1926). Typically, self-centeredness is a common trait of preschoolers and is not due to "selfishness or reprehensible callousness. Rather, it is a developmental stage, and . . . he [the child] is in the process of learning to decenter and see the world from another's vantage point" (Hendrick 1975).

There is lack of agreement as to how children become socialized (Parke 1972). Apparently they do so by identifying with and imitating others and by being reinforced (praised or rewarded) for social behaviors that are acceptable and desirable in our society. They behave like older children and adults, especially if the model appears to be loving and powerful (Bandura and Huston 1961; Mischel and Grusec 1966).

You can be reassured that when you send a *double message* (when your words say one thing and your actions say another), your child will be more likely to follow your actions than your words (Rosenhan 1972). Try to *do* as you would have him do, and reduce the number of lectures. If beans are served for dinner and you make a distasteful face and pass them on while telling your child to "eat all your beans," he will make the same distasteful face and pass the beans right on. No matter how much you say how good beans are and how strong they will make your child, if beans aren't good enough for you, they aren't good enough for him.

If your preschooler does something good that you notice, approve of, and acknowledge through words or actions, he feels encouraged to repeat this type of behavior (Allen, Hart, Buell, Harris, and Wolf 1964; Horowitz 1967). If your child does something bad that you disapprove of and if you then punish or suppress the behavior, he tends not to repeat it (Parke 1972b). You influence your child's behavior by your reactions—either positive or negative—to what he does, so it is important that you assume an active, guiding role (Hendrick 1975). You need to provide a good model for your child, and your relationship should be based on mutual respect and acceptance (Bandura and Huston 1961; Mussen and Parker 1965).

It is important for your child to see and interact with models of both sexes. Since women are most involved with young children, girls almost always have a same-sex model to follow, but boys also need same-sex models from fathers, neighbors, teachers, and others, and you should be sure such models are provided. Children also need to identify with a good model of the opposite sex.

When your preschooler wants something (attention, assistance, or possession), he wants it *NOW*; the need is "immediate, intense, and personal" (Hendrick 1975). Being unable to wait for delayed gratification, being self-centered, and not having reasoning skills or social techniques, your child wants *action* to fill his needs. All of this is part of your child's growth pattern, so be patient.

Competence

At Harvard University a study was conducted to determine the qualities of low- and high-competency children. Researchers found that social competence such as language skills, good use of time, and good attitude develops during the second and third years of life (White 1972).

Mothers of high-competency children provided:

- more freedom for the child to use large muscles and make gross motor movements
- more live language opportunities for both listening and talking
- more objects to handle and look at, with encouragement to explore those objects

In other words, these mothers responded to the needs of the child and had a positive attitude toward life themselves.

On the other hand, low-competency children tend to have mothers who

- use more playpens and gates
- let the television provide the child's only language stimulus
- remove objects from the child's sight and touch (thereby discouraging exploration)
- meet their own needs more than the child's
- have a negative attitude toward life

Mothers of high-competency children teach their children at "teachable moments," which are spontaneous and opportunistic (things that just happen are made interesting and important); they exhibit enjoyment in and with their children. Two of their most identifiable resources are *energy* and *patience;* although they spend less than ten percent of their time interacting with their infants, the *quality* of their interaction is more important than the *quantity* (or the amount of time spent) (Brophy 1975).

Remember that if your toddler doesn't develop autonomy, shame and doubt will take over; if your preschool child doesn't develop initiative, guilt will grow. These negative feelings develop when your child doesn't have the opportunity to express his independence. Some parents even capitalize on such feelings to control behavior without realizing the dangers they introduce in personality development (Erikson 1963). Parents who try to control their children through *negative psychology*—telling children to do the opposite of what they should do, because that is what they'll do anyway—confuse and retard good personal development.

As your child pushes toward autonomy and initiative, you should develop positive attitudes toward this striving. In other words, your relationship to your child during his preschool years is related to his achievement in the elementary school years (Smart and Smart 1973; Crandall 1964). Parents who are loving, consistent, reasonable, demanding, and respectful of their children's decisions have children who are social and independent (Baumrind 1967). These parents provide limits and guidelines while encouraging their children to develop initiative.

Prejudice

Many adults think that the young child is not aware of nor concerned with problems of prejudice and discrimination. This is not so. Children as young as three years of age respond to different skin color (Landreth and Johnson 1953; Morland 1972; Werner and Evans 1971), and these responses definitely increase from ages three to five. The fact that children are able to discriminate is not necessarily an indication that they will reject those with a different skin color.

How you respond to members of minority groups will definitely affect your child's attitude. You can help fight prejudice by discussing differences from your child (skin color, cultures, traditions) and also by pointing out similarities (bodily and psychological needs, cooperative work) (Hendrick 1975). Further research is needed to determine more exactly what promotes and what prevents racial prejudice in young children.

Some suggested ways to reduce or prevent prejudice in your family include the following (adapted from a list prepared by Clark 1963):

- Identify a person or family of a different ethnic heritage or minority group in your community. Get acquainted with the family and try to have a good time together (go to the park or zoo, entertain or visit them, or take them a treat).
- Treat others as you would like to be treated: use common courtesies and proper titles.
- Think carefully about what you are going to say in these situations so that you don't make some unkind statement.
- When you hear rumors, demand proof of the statements; never spread unsupported ideas.
- Use only terms that show acceptance and respect.
- Avoid telling or repeating stories or jokes that are unkind toward other ethnic groups.
- Welcome and accept families and individuals from other cultures or minority groups.
- Learn some interesting ethnic customs or ideas that you could incorporate into your family.
- Take your child along when you patronize businesses that are run by people of different ethnic origins, and introduce him to the owners if possible.

Guidelines for Parents

If you are wondering how you can help your child's social progress, here are a few simple but effective ways:

- Help your child learn to be generous through sharing equipment, experiences, and others' time. Show good examples and use verbal clarification. Establish a guideline for sharing: let your child use something as long as he wants, or for a certain length of time, or under certain conditions. Remember that your child needs to possess something before he can share. Help your child understand the total cycle of activity (preparing, using, and cleaning up) and spend individual, uninterrupted time with just him.
- Help your child understand the feelings of others as much as he is able to. Role play, ask him simple questions, or discuss situations and individuals.

- Help your child serve others. Show him how he could help others and how helping makes everyone feel.
- Help your child show respect for others. Each person has rights, responsibilities, and privileges. Everyone wants to know that his rights will be protected, just as he needs to protect the rights of others. Teach your child that respect is a mutual thing.
- Help your child develop good social techniques; teach him that co-operation and compromise are better than competition. Show him ways and teach him verbal methods of interacting appropriately with others. Show him how to trade for a desired toy, for example, or help your child use words that aid cooperation—"If you put away the square blocks and I put away the round ones, we'll soon be through."
- Help your child develop and appreciate friendships. By the time your child is five years old, he will be spending more than half of his available playtime with other children (Valentine 1956) and will develop strong bonds with certain of those children (Green 1933).
- Help your child decide on and utilize behavior that is appropriate for his sex and age, but give him opportunities for activities that are characteristic of the opposite sex. Your child needs to develop all the interests and abilities that he can, even if they are tradition-ally sex role-linked. (The above seven suggestions were adapted from Hendrick 1975.)
- Help your child establish rules for behavior. Using some guidelines, together you can identify simple rules and rationale. You can in-crease the rules in complexity as he advances in experiences and development. (Rules can include simple things like when and who should feed the pet or what happens when your child misbehaves.)
- Help your child work through questions, experiences, and con-cerns by providing the necessary props, time, and space for sus-tained dramatic play. Listen to his concerns and comments so that you can help clarify his misconceptions and can aid in further so-cial development.

Discipline

Discipline (training that develops self-control, character, or orderliness and efficiency) can be accomplished when parents and child both work together in love, patience, and understanding. The goal is to build a good reliable control from *within* the person.

Sometimes it is hard to understand some things the young child does; but sometimes it is even hard to understand ourselves. We often don't know the cause of or the response for our own behavior, and we can't figure out why we sometimes act one way and sometimes act an-other way. (See also the discussion on "Anger, Aggression, and Hostil-ity" in Chapter Three.)

Causes of Misbehavior

According to Hymes (1960) there are four causes of misbehavior. The first is *growth*. Because a child is changing, he will want to do more and more things; because the child's body will be telling him to be active and explorative, the child may go out of bounds while striving for the independence that is essential to growing up. When your child gets out of line, you have three viable courses of action: (1) *tolerate* the behavior, even if you have to look away from or tune out inappropriate behavior; (2) *channel* the behavior, telling your child *where* he can do certain things (he can cry or shout in the bedroom but not in the grocery store) or *what* he can do (he can cut the paper but not the curtains); or (3) set a limit and *stop* the actions.

A second cause for misbehavior may be a *need* your child has (a need for affection, approval, belonging, or bigness, for example). This cause does not pass in time, as does growth; instead, it generally intensifies. You should feed your child's need (for attention and approval, for example). To encourage appropriate behavior, help him feel wanted and worthwhile. Some good ways of feeding your child's needs are through dramatic play and creative expression.

The *situation* or *environment* is the third possible cause of misbehavior. It's fairly easy to change the situation, removing temptations for misbehavior. Put away things your child is not supposed to have— Daddy's tools, prized possessions, and so on. Experiment with the environment to make it better suited to your child: change his routine, change the arrangement of your child's room, or rearrange the placement of materials (don't put the scissors near the new encyclopedia).

If the cause of misbehavior is not one of the above three, perhaps your child just *doesn't know any better.* How did your son know the cat would drown in a tub of water? He was just trying to teach her to swim like his dog. How did your daughter know that sand would clog the plumbing? She was just trying to wash out her new bucket. Times like these let you do some of your best teaching. Capitalize on these teachable moments when your child is interested and trying to accomplish something. He is not deliberately being destructive, but he just lacks knowledge and experience.

If you want to help your child behave in a certain way, try to praise him honestly and often for the good things he does. This keeps your child moving in a positive direction and encourages repetition of good behavior. So often your child hears limiting words like *don't, quit,* or *stop* that leave him dangling in the air without any direction. But when you tell your child what to *do,* he can continue to fulfill the goal in a manner that is acceptable to you. Here's a simple example: suppose you are both sitting at the lunch table and your child starts to pour his own milk. If you say, "Don't spill the milk," your child is likely to become defensive, overcautious, and even rebellious. *He* wants to be in control. But if you say, "Pour your milk up to the line on the glass," your child has a direction and a goal to work toward. Then if he spills the milk, kindly say, "Here's a sponge to wipe up the milk." Don't say, "I *knew* you would spill," or "Can't you do *anything* right?" Both of these last comments reflect negatively upon your child and his abilities; he is not going to try anything new if he is always in fear of failure.

Self-assertiveness is part of being a four-year-old. Boys usually become physically daring or start bragging; girls often resort to bossing and tattling. Cultural expectations are different for boys and girls—with boys using direct physical methods and girls using more indirect methods—but how much of this difference is due to biology and/or culture has not yet been determined (Hendrick 1975). Because assertiveness can help a child's attempts at initiative, it should not be entirely crushed.

Your child should behave within appropriate guidelines, but should have some flexibility. Remember that all children are different; some are naturally calm, while others are more assertive and fiery.

Establishing Limits

Recognize that limits on your child's behavior have value; they should be designed to help his growth and development, to protect him from harm and danger, and they should be reasonable for your child's age and experience. If you will let your child help set the limits ("Where do you think you should paint?"), he is much more apt to adhere to them, but externally imposed limits retard progress toward internal control. That's what discipline is all about—helping your child accept and develop self-control. Make sure the limits are

- Clear and flexible but consistent and maintained.
- "Testable," so that your child knows when to push and when to stop.
- Suitable to your child and to the situation.
- Respectful of your child.
- Helpful in building relationships.
- Helpful in developing your child's self-control (Read 1976).

Remember that "self-control depends on ego strength as well as on the conscience, and self-esteem makes the ego stronger" (Hendrick 1975).

If your child continually misbehaves, discuss the behavior with him in language and with experiences that are easy for him to understand. Warn your child of possible consequences. Then if the misbehavior continues, you may need to remove your child from the situation until he can act properly; if this happens, help your child return to the situation and be successful. (Your child may deliberately bump into others with his trike. After continual warnings, say, "If you bump into anyone again, your turn on the trike will be over." The incident reoccurs. Remove your child—physically, if necessary—and put the trike away. Explain the situation to your child, and get him interested in another activity. At another time discuss the rules for trike-riding and bring the trike out again. Compliment your child on his good driving skills.) If you are a *controlling* person—maintaining control through authoritarianism or permissiveness—you will find it difficult to deal with some of your child's aggressive behavior (Hendrick 1975).

In a study of nursery school children, those who were "self-controlled and friendly on the one hand, and self-reliant, explorative, and self-assertive on the other hand" were found to have parents who were consistent, loving, and demanding. Although parents respected their children as individuals with the right to be independent, they took and maintained a firm stand on decisions, gave reasons for their decisions, and balanced warmth and acceptance with high control. Their demands were clearly communicated to their children. Children can and do benefit from restricted freedom without the loss of individual autonomy or self-assertiveness (Baumrind 1967; Coopersmith 1967).

Reinforcement

It is easy to reinforce desirable behavior (to make it stronger or more frequent). Whenever your child does something good or right, let him know immediately that you are pleased either through *honest* verbal praise, by appropriate gestures (smiling or nodding), or by granting him special privileges. When he *first* begins doing something you like, reinforce every good action; then gradually reinforce only occasional actions. As your child's good behavior continues, expect and reward improvement (Becker 1971).

You may have become so preoccupied with negative behavior that you fail to comment on what your child does well or right. You may need to recondition yourself by making and posting some little reminders throughout the house: "Love-Fear" reminds you to get good behavior from your child because of love, not because of fear; "Praise" reminds you to look for and catch him being "good" rather than waiting for and punishing his misbehavior; "Think of the good" reminds you to look for his good behavior. You could also make a list of praising words and phrases that you could read over and practice daily: "Good," "You really tried hard," "You can do lots of things if you just try," "That was a good job," "That's a new (or different) way to do it," "Thanks for _____," "Very clever," "Right," "That took a lot of thinking," "What a fun way," "How interesting," "It was nice of you to do that," and others. You may want to practice some nonverbal methods, too, such as smiling, nodding, laughing, or winking; getting closer to your child's level by sitting or kneeling; or displaying physical contact like touching, hugging, holding your child, holding hands, or leaning against each other. These methods tell your child a lot about himself and about your relationship.

When your child does something you like, it will help if you briefly describe his good act ("That was so nice of you to pick up the baby's rattle."). Your child needs the verbalization at first; later he will get your message through nonverbal means such as a smile or a hug. Your child also needs immediate and tangible reinforcers (such as having privileges, being able to make something, or going somewhere). It will be some time before he gets much value out of delayed reinforcers.

Parents need to learn how to select and use reinforcers. All children are not motivated by the same things, so it is important to identify those that appeal to a specific child. Praise is used so often that you may have to look hard and long to find child-specific reinforcement. Some children respond to food; some respond to privileges; and still others respond to attention. There is considerable evidence that socially acceptable responses can be learned as a result of reinforcement (Allen, Hart, Buell, Harris, and Wolf 1964; Horowitz 1967). This reinforcement can be *negative* (punishment) (Parke 1972a) or *positive* (recognition and praise) from either external or internal sources (Hendrick 1975).

Before disciplining your child, find something to say that is positive and that builds your relationship. Then your child will feel accepted even though he must be disciplined, he will be attentive, and you will have a chance to cool off. Show respect for your child's feelings and activities, too. Sometimes he is so involved that it is very difficult to leave and do as you request. A few minutes' warning to allow your child to finish a project or come to a good stopping place will make it easier for him to leave what he is doing. Your child will also find it easier to move from one activity to another if what you are requesting is also of value or interest to him. Give your child a choice when appropriate and then be able to accept his selection.

Punishment

Punishment is the attempt to reduce or weaken unacceptable behavior. You should use it to accomplish at least four things: (1) to make it impossible for your child to avoid or escape the punisher, (2) to prevent a negative relationship from developing between you and your child, (3) to reduce the need for future punishment, and (4) to avoid providing your child with a negative or aggressive model of behavior (Becker 1971).

Although you should use reinforcement of good behavior whenever you can, you may find the need for punishment if there is a lack of any good behavior to reinforce, a question of safety for your child and others, or when outside influences (peer group pressures or growth needs) are more powerful. As with reinforcement, there are some rules to follow with punishment: (1) give it immediately following the misbehavior; (2) provide some clear way of restoring any reinforcers taken away; (3) use a method of warning; (4) administer it in a calm, matter-of-fact way; (5) reinforce incompatible behavior (the child is unable to hit someone if he is using his hands in making something); and (6) be consistent (Becker 1971).

The sooner the punishment follows the negative behavior (*now* rather than "when Daddy gets home" or "when I finish what I am doing") and the more intense the punishment, the more effective it will be. However, the timing of the punishment is not as important as the intensity. Punishment accompanied by rationale is more effective than either rationale or punishment alone in correcting inappropriate behavior; but reasoning added to late-timed punishment increases its effectiveness. Young children respond better to physical punishment—a slap on the hand or the rear—because of their inability to understand words; older children respond better to verbal methods. Consistency on the part of parents is important in establishing behavior patterns; inconsistency builds up your child's resistance to your future attempts to extinguish or suppress his undesirable behavior (Parke 1972).

Some cautions about using punishment include the following:

- Don't be a model of aggressive behavior. Often parents spank children while saying, "How many times have I told you not to hit someone?" This situation shows that power, often desired by the young child, comes from aggressiveness.
- Instead of building relationships, punishment can destroy them.
- The child who is continually punished may withdraw from interaction and activities because of a fear of failure or punishment.
- A child could be physically or emotionally scarred by punishment. (Child abuse is a serious problem in our country.)
- "It is unlikely that a socialization program based solely on punishment would be very effective; the child needs to be taught new appropriate responses in addition to learning to suppress unacceptable forms of behavior" (Parke 1972).

Guidelines for Parents

See if you can determine the cause of your child's immediate misbehavior:

- Could it be due to some physical or environmental reason such as low blood sugar, illness, or upset in the family?
- Is your child trying to do something, but does he lack the needed motor skills?
- Is his environment frustrating?
- Does your child have the social and emotional techniques he needs to express his desires?
- Does your child have the language abilities and the problem-solving means to express himself?

If you can determine the cause of the misbehavior and remedy it, your child's behavior will often change.

Try remedies such as these:

- Reduce situations that frustrate your child; help him learn how to deal with them in a constructive way.
- Step in before your child reaches the explosion level. If he must pound on something, substitute a pounding bench or a bag for his baby sister.
- Give your child props so he can express his feelings (dress-up clothing, clay, tools that work, or a stick horse).
- Provide plenty of time and space for play and eliminate distractions.

In a nutshell, discipline will be most effective when it is administered by a loving person, when reward or punishment immediately follow the act, when reasons and rationale for the behavior have been established, when discipline is based on your child's developmental growth and needs, when you are consistent but flexible in your expectations and discipline, and when your child clearly understands what is expected.

Guidance is summed up compactly and beautifully in four steps (Waring 1955):

- Approval fosters values.
- Help stimulates abilities.
- Respect encourages self-respect.
- Affection gives security.

References for Societal Interaction and Prejudice:

Allen, K., B. Hart, J. S. Buell, F. R. Harris, and M. M. Wolf, "Effects of Social Reinforcement on Isolate Behavior of a Nursery School Child," *Child Development,* 35(2), 1964, 511–518.

Bandura, A., *Aggression: A Social Learning Analysis,* Englewood Cliffs, N.J.: Prentice-Hall, Inc., 1973.

Bandura, A., and A. C. Huston, "Identification as a Process of Incidental Learning," *Journal of Abnormal Social Psychology,* 63, 1961, 311–318.

Baumrind, D., "Socialization and Instrumental Competence in Young Children," in W. W. Hartup, ed., *The Young Child: Reviews of Research,* vol. 2, Washington, D.C., NAEYC, 1972.

Baumrind, D., and A. E. Black, "Socialization Practices Associated with Dimensions of Competence in Preschool Boys and Girls," *Child Development,* 38, 1967, 291–327.

Borke, H., "Interpersonal Perception of Young Children: Egocentrism or Empathy?" *Developmental Psychology,* 5(2), 1971, 263–269.

Bronfenbrenner, Urie, ed., *Influences on Human Development,* Hinsdale, Ill.: The Dryden Press, Inc., 1972.

Brophy, Jere E., Thomas L. Good, and Shari E. Nedler, *Teaching in the Preschool,* New York: Harper and Row Publishers, 1975.

Clark, H. B., *Prejudice and Your Child,* 2nd ed., Boston: Beacon Press, 1963.

Cratty, B. J., *Perceptual and Motor Development in Infants and Children,* New York: Macmillan, 1970.

Dawe, H. C., "An Analysis of Two Hundred Quarrels of Preschool Children," *Child Development,* 5, 1934, 139–157.

Flavell, J. H., "Role-taking and Communication Skills in Children," *Young Children, 21,* 1966, 164–177.

Gordon, Ira J., "Parenting, Teaching and Child Development," *Young Children,* March 1976, pp. 173–182.

Green, E. H., "Group Play and Quarreling Among Preschool Children," *Child Development, 4,* 1933, 302–307.

Greenberg, P. J., "Competition in Children: An Experimental Study," *American Journal of Psychology, 44,* 1932, 221–249.

Griffin, L., *Multi-ethnic Books for Young Children: Annotated Bibliography for Parents and Teachers,* Washington, D.C.: National Associa. for the Ed. of Young Children (NAEYC), n.d.

Griffiths, Ruth, *A Study of Imagination in Early Childhood,* London: Kegan, Paul, Trench, Trubner, 1935.

Hartup, W. W., ed., *The Young Child, Review of Research,* vol. 2, Washington, D.C.: NAEYC, 1972.

Hartup, W. W., and B. Coates, "Imitation of a Peer as a Function of Reinforcement from the Peer Group and Rewardingness of the Model," *Child Development, 38,* 1967, 1003–1016.

Hartup, Willard W., and Nancy L. Smothergill, eds., *The Young Child: Review of Research,* vol. I, Washington, D.C.: NAEYC, 1967.

Hendrick, Joanne, *The Whole Child: New Trends in Early Education,* St. Louis: The C. V. Mosby Company, 1975.

Hoffman, M. L., "Childrearing Practices and Moral Development: Generalizations from Empirical Research," *Child Development,* 34, 1963, 295–318.

Horowitz, F. D., "Social Reinforcement Effects on Child Behavior," in W. W. Hartup and N. L. Smothergill, eds., *The Young Child: Review of Research,* vol. I, Washington, D.C.:NAEYC, 1967.

Hymes, James L., *Understanding Your Child,* Englewood Cliffs, N.J.: Prentice-Hall, 1952.

Landreth, C., and B. C. Johnson, "Young Children's Responses to a Picture Inset Test Designed to Reveal Reactions to Persons of Different Skin Color," *Child Development, 24,* 1953, 63–80.

Latimer, B. I., ed., *Starting Out Right: Choosing Books about Black People for Young Children, Preschool Through Third Grade,* Wisconsin Department of Public Instruction, 1972. Reprinted: Washington, D.C.: Day Care and Child Development Council of America, 1972.

Lillie, David L., *Early Childhood Education,* Chicago: Science Research Association, 1975.

Maccoby, E. E., ed., *The Development of Sex Differences,* Stanford, Calif.: Stanford University Press, 1966.

Maudry, M., and M. Nekula, "Social Relations Between Children of the Same Age During the First Two Years of Life," *Journal of Genetic Psychology, 54,* 1939, 193–215.

Midlarsky, E., and J. H. Bryan, "Training Charity in Children," *Journal of Personality and Social Psychology, 5,* 1967, 405–415.

Mischel, W., and J. Grusec, "Determinants of the Rehearsal and Transmission of Neutral and Aversive Behaviors," *Journal of Personality and Social Psychology, 3,* 1966, 197–205.

Morland, J. K., "Racial Acceptance and Preference of Nursery School Children in a Southern City," in A. R. Brown, ed., *Prejudice in Children,* Springfield, Ill.: Charles C. Thomas, Publisher, 1972.

Mussen, P., and A. Parker, "Mother Nurturance and Girls' Incidental Imitative Learning," *Journal of Personality and Social Psychology, 2,* 1965, 94–97.

Parke, R. D., ed., *Recent Trends in Social Learning Theory,* New York: Academic Press, Inc., 1972(a).

Parke, R. D., "Some Effects of Punishment on Children's Behavior," in W. W. Hartup, ed., *The Young Child: Reviews of Research,* vol. 2, Washington, D.C.: NAEYC, 1972(b).

Peck, R. F., and R. J. Havighurst, *The Psychology of Character Development,* New York: Wiley, 1960.

Piaget, J., *The Language and Thought of the Child,* New York: Harcourt Brace Jovanovich, Inc., 1926.

Rosenhan, D., "Prosocial Behavior of Children," in W. W. Hartup, ed., *The Young Child, Reviews of Research,* vol. 2, Washington, D.C.: NAEYC, 1972.

Rutherford, P. and P. Mussen, "Generosity in Nursery School Boys," *Child Development, 39,* 1968, 755–765.

Siegel, A. E., L. M. Stolz, E. A. Hitchcock, and J. M. Adamson, "Dependence and Independence in the Children of Working Mothers," *Child Development, 30,* 1959, 533–546.

Smart, Mollie, and Russell C. Smart, *Preschool Children: Development and Relationships,* New York: Macmillan, 1973.

Smedslund, J., "Les origines Sociales de la Centration," in F. Bresson and M. de montmalin, eds., *Psychologie et epistemologie Genetiques,* Paris: Dunod, 1966.

Stevenson, H. W., "Studies of Racial Awareness in Young Children," in W. W. Hartup and N. L. Smothergill, eds., *The Young Child: Reviews of Research,* Washington, D.C.: NAEYC, 1967.

Stevenson, H. W., and N. G. Stevenson, "Social Interaction in an Interracial Nursery School," *Genetic Psychology Monographs, 61,* 1960, 41–75.

Stevenson, H. W., and E. C. Stewart, "A Developmental Study of Racial Awareness in Young Children," *Child Development,* 29, 1958, 400–409.

Stoltz, L. M., "Effects of Maternal Employment on Children: Evidence from Research," *Child Development,* 31, 1960, 749–782.

Sutton-Smith, B., *Child Psychology.* Englewood Cliffs, N.J.: Prentice-Hall, Inc., 1973.

Thompson, G. G., "The Social and Emotional Development of Preschool Children under Two Types of Educational Programs," *Psychological Monographs,* 56(5), 1944, 1–29.

Valentine, C. W., *The Normal Child and His Abnormalities,* 3rd ed., Baltimore: Penguin Books, Inc., 1956.

Werner, N. E., and I. M. Evans, "Perception of Prejudice in Mexican-American Preschool Children," in N. N. Wagner, and M. J. Haug, *Chicano: Social and Psychological Perspectives,* St. Louis: The C. V. Mosby Company, 1971.

White, Burton, "Fundamental Early Environmental Influences on the Development of Competence," in M. Meyer, ed., *Third Symposium on Learning: Cognitive Learning,* Bellingham, Wash.: Western Washington State College, 1972.

Wood, Mary Margaret, *The Rutland Center Model for Treating Emotionally Disturbed Children,* Athens, Georgia: Rutland Center Technical Assistance Office, 1972.

References for Discipline:

Allen, K. B., Hart, J. S. Buell, F. R. Harris, and M. M. Wolf, "Effects of Social Reinforcement on Isolate Behavior of a Nursery School Child," *Child Development,* 35(2), 1964, 511–518.

Bandura, A., *Aggression: A Social Learning Analysis,* Englewood Cliffs, N.J.: Prentice-Hall, Inc., 1973.

Baumrind, D., "Some Thoughts About Childrearing," in Urie Bronfenbrenner, ed., *Influences on Human Development,* Hinsdale, Ill.: The Dryden Press, Inc., 1972, pp. 396–409.

Baumrind, D., "Child Care Practices Anteceding Three Patterns of Preschool Behavior," *Genetic Psychology Monographs,* 1967, 75, 43–88.

Baumrind, D., and A. E. Black, "Socialization Practices Associated with Dimensions of Competence in Preschool Boys and Girls," *Child Development,* 38, 1967, 291–327.

Becker, Wesley C., *Parents Are Teachers,* Champaign, Ill.: Research Press Company, 1971.

Bronfenbrenner, Urie, ed., *Influences on Human Development,* Hinsdale, Ill.: The Dryden Press, Inc., 1972.

Coopersmith, S., *The Antecedents of Self-Esteem,* San Francisco: Freeman, 1967.

Crandall, V. C., "Achievement Behavior in Young Children," *Young Children,* 20, 1964, 77–90.

Glueck, S., and E. Glueck, *Unraveling Juvenile Delinquency,* Cambridge, Mass.: Harvard University Press, 1950.

Hendrick, Joanne, *The Whole Child: New Trends in Early Education,* St. Louis: The C. V. Mosby Company, 1975.

Horowitz, F. D., "Social Reinforcement Effects on Child Behavior," in W. W. Hartup and N. L. Smothergill, eds., *The Young Child: Reviews of Research,* vol. I, Washington, D.C.: NAEYC, 1967.

Hymes, James L., *Understanding Your Child,* Englewood Cliffs, N.J.: Prentice-Hall, Inc., 1960.

Kagan, Jerome, *Understanding Children: Behavior, Motives and Thought,* New York: Harcourt Brace Jovanovich, Inc., 1971.

Lorenz, K., *On Aggression,* translated by M. K. Wilson, New York: Harcourt Brace Jovanovich, Inc., 1966.

McCord, W., J. McCord, and A. Howard, "Familiar Correlates of Aggression in Non-Delinquent Male Children," *Journal of Abnormal Social Psychology,* 1961, *62,* 79–93.

Parke, Ross D., "Some Effects of Punishment on Children's Behavior," in W. W. Hartup, ed., *The Young Child: Reviews of Research,* vol. 2, Washington, D.C.: 1972, pp. 264–283. Also in Urie Bronfenbrenner, ed., *Influences on Human Development,* Hinsdale, Ill.: Dryden Press, Inc., 1972, pp. 378–96.

Smart, Mollie, and Russell C. Smart, *Preschool Children: Development and Relationships,* New York: Macmillan, 1973.

Waring, Ethel, *Principles for Child Guidance,* Cornell Extension Bulletin #420, New York: New York State College of Home Economics, 1955.

Five

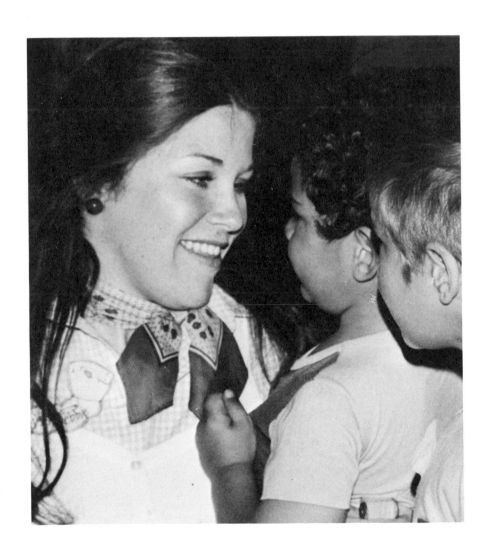

Moral Development

A Note from Your Preschooler

Dear Mom and Dad,

I don't know much about good and bad yet. But I know that if I do something and you spank me, I don't want to do it again—very soon. My mind is starting to tell me what's right and wrong, but sometimes my body doesn't listen. It's hard for me to understand that what I do can make something else happen—if I touch the hot stove, I get burned. I just can't think such things through yet.

I want to please you and other people very much. Sometimes I can do it, but other times everything I do is wrong. One day I polished your new table with cleansing cream—but you got very mad. Another day my big sister told me to take some things out of your special cupboard. When I did, she said I had done a good thing, but you were so mad at me you sent me to my room. Things like this are hard for me to understand.

Sometimes I can't tell the difference between real and pretend, so I lie or tell stories. I don't know the difference, so don't spank me for it; I will do better later.

I will try to do and be what you want. Sometimes it is hard because I have to learn to do things by *myself.*

Love,
Your Preschooler

Introduction

The preschool child's ideas of right and wrong depend upon his experiences, his socialization, and his intellectual abilities. The first two years of his life are spent mainly in learning through sensorimotor (combining the five senses with action) activities, and the child has no true concepts at all. He continues activities that are reinforcing (that are encouraged or rewarded by others) and forgets those that are discouraged or punished. So even though a child's behavior is somewhat predictable, the child has no general sense of right and wrong. The preschool child is actually in a premoral stage of development (Kohlberg 1964).

Because your child attaches personal significance to important people in his life, he wants to please them—especially you, his parents. When you're happy, your child is happy, too. He often doesn't understand why he is permitted to do some things but not others. Getting clues from your reactions to his behavior, your child notes that when you say *good* or *big,* you often smile. He will try to remember to do things that make you say these words.

Lying

The preschooler knows that you don't accept lying, but he doesn't view it quite as adults do; his thinking capacity is not that well developed. Suppose you see your daughter hit a vase with a ball that you had told her not to throw in the house. But she knows that balls are for *throwing,* and she doesn't think about balls breaking things, as you do. Your child knows that saying "I'm sorry" seems to make *you* feel better, but it doesn't really change the situation for her. She still doesn't see why you are so upset; she *told* you she didn't break the vase. She was just throwing—the *ball* did the breaking.

It takes time for your child to develop the mental ability to think things through, and you need to develop patience with these immaturities. Having lived a long time in society, you have developed desirable moral qualities, but your child's experiences have been very limited.

You can make your child promise to never lie again, but he won't understand that, either. It's going to take him until he is an adolescent to develop "a truly systematic and · internally integrated morality" (Brophy 1975). Until then your child will repeat what you have said about right and wrong, but he will not take it seriously or question it; he simply doesn't have the needed intellectual abilities. Trying to instill insight and responsibility in your child when he cannot comprehend them will be as useless as treating him like a baby when he is sixteen years old.

Behavioral Changes

In general, at age three a child obeys only when he is being watched. At four he begins to internalize your demands, judging other people by the results of their acts and not by their intentions, but realizing the difference between intentional and unintentional rule-breaking for himself. According to Piaget (an expert on childhood who is read by most education students and many parents), moral realism is strict adherence and obedience to a rule—with results that are evaluated by the motives. The preschooler can judge what a person does only by the *results* of the action (not by a person's motives or intentions), and he can judge only from his limited point of view. When asked which was worse, a child who accidentally broke five cups or a child who deliberately broke one cup, the preschooler will say the first child is worse, because more cups were broken! It will be a while before he can be classed as having developed "moral realism."

The child also has some early feelings of guilt and may even express them verbally—"That wasn't nice." By age six the conscience is fairly well internalized, there are definite feelings of guilt, and the child uses language in evaluating his actions (Smart and Smart 1973). Before school age, the conscience will develop slowly, but two things will help it progress: (1) a good, supportive, affectionate relationship between you and your child, and (2) his ability to reason (Mussen, Conger, and Kagan 1969; Sutton-Smith 1973).

You may be displeased with your child's tattling, but you might as well get used to it, because it is a natural stage in his conscience development, especially during the fourth year of life. Unless someone's safety or health is endangered, send your child back to his playmates to resolve the situation. If you *must* get involved, do so in a nonjudgmental manner. Chances are that you don't know the circumstances, although everyone will be willing to tell them to you. If you do take sides, somebody will be sure to yell, "Unfair!"

Between the third and sixth years, your child begins to take some of the expectations of society onto himself; when he has your loving support, this process will be easier. Your child will accept your role in acknowledging acceptable behavior and in disapproving unacceptable behavior. If your child can adapt his behavior and can evaluate it, he will also be able to accept your disappointment. Your child knows that you are showing him that you think he can live up to your expectations. Your child believes in his ability, too—even though it hurts when you disapprove (Smart and Smart 1973).

Developing Values

During the preschool period your child doesn't have any values of his own. You will probably try to impose yours—a good idea only up to a point. As soon as your preschooler begins to have the ability to make his own decisions, you can help him carefully evaluate things. Your child needs to develop his own value system based on reason and good judgment; the many values you want to pass on because of your family or cultural heritage must also be understood by your child. Help your child do things for the right reasons rather than because he is told to do them.

Work is one of those assets valued by our society. A child as young as three or four years of age can accept the fact that work brings benefits. If he helps you now with household tasks, you can have fun together later, after the beds are made—or he can even earn some coins for his bank. It feels good to help someone—your child feels bigger, more important, and independent.

The two of you may disagree on what *work* really is. You may think all your child does is play, but actually *everything* is work to him—although not in the negative sense. Play—the child's work—is how he learns about the world. Doing things for himself and for others returns a sense of accomplishment and strength as the child assumes adult roles.

Here are seven *Cs* to practice that will help your child like and appreciate work:

- Cooperation—let your child help you with jobs you like to do, and you help him with jobs that are big or unpleasant for him.
- Completion—let your child see the end of the job in sight.
- Competition—give your child jobs he can do successfully.
- Criticism—expect your child to do a good job within his capabilities, and approve of the results (perfection will come later).
- Conditions—give your child guidelines as to how and when to work and provide good tools for him to work with, but leave some room for individual variation.
- Congeniality—have a good attitude toward things that have to be done; maybe offer the choice of trading jobs with your child.
- Complexity—give your child some easy and some harder jobs, but always give him a variety. (Something you always do may look more appealing, or your child may think he always gets the undesirable jobs).

Since you will be very influential in which values your child adopts or rejects, be honest in your interaction. For example, try to value things that are a part of your child (such as a creative drawing, a block structure, or an original idea), and play down those things that are stereotyped (such as behavior that is copied from someone else or an answer that you expect as "right"). Because the things you value now or in the past may not be in vogue with the current generation, look at your *own* values with a critical eye and an open mind, but do help your child to understand and value some of the things you hold sacred: religion, honesty, morality, character, cultural and subcultural traditions, family unity, and service to others, for example.

Sometimes the earning and spending of money provides a source of conflict between parent and child. With the young preschooler, you could have an understanding and an arrangement to resolve this conflict early for both of you. Because your child doesn't yet know the value of money or even how to spend it, he needs your help. Perhaps your child could get a small allowance or earn some money, and then be allowed to spend it however he wishes. Don't be too harsh if your child buys something impractical or if he wastes his money. Early experiences like this can help later when your child has more money, more desires, and more ability to make decisions. How did you learn about money—through lectures or "the hard way?"

Also teach your child some honest concepts about sex. Use the proper names for the parts of his body or for his bodily functions so that he doesn't have to try to interpret the meanings of all those different expressions ("potty," "tinkle," and "wet," for example.) When your child asks questions about sex, just give an honest, short answer to his question. When he is ready for more, he will ask.

It's important for you to encourage your child to have a positive attitude about his body. When a preschooler stares at another person's unclothed body, he is just trying to get concepts of femaleness and maleness in mind; he is *not* really being "bad" or immoral. Actually it's healthy for him to see another person's body and to have his curiosity satisfied before he gets much older. Bathing with a brother or sister or a parent can answer many of the preschooler's questions before they are asked. A calm, reassuring attitude on your part will really help. Your attitudes about sex will probably become your child's.

Don't get caught in the "where did I come from?" trap. Find out what it is that your child is asking, and then give him a simple answer. He may not want as much information as you think he does. Your casual acceptance of his questions and your *honest* answers will cause your child to return to you for more information later; your anxious, lengthy, inaccurate answers will send him elsewhere.

Language, experience, and personal development will help your child establish a moral code. Assist him by providing him with the opportunities he will need, but also be understanding of his questioning and reasoning.

Guidelines for Parents

You can help your young child achieve moral maturity in several ways:

- Let your child participate in democratic discussions to organize ideas and actions. Through verbalization your child can evaluate his actions—such evaluation is the foundation for developing guilt, which is evident at four or five years of age (Smart and Smart 1973).
- Reward the behavior you want your child to continue, and ignore the behavior you want discontinued. If your child repeats undesired behavior, stop and evaluate what caused it, and then change the situation.
- Interact with your child in a positive rather than a negative way: tell him what he *can* do rather than what he *can't* do.
- Give your child a choice when there *really* is a choice.
- Establish important limits and enforce them.
- Show respect for your child as an individual by doing these things:
  — warning him about the need to stop or change an activity
  — valuing your child's ideas and letting him try them out
  — listening attentively when he is talking

— providing opportunities and activities appropriate for his developmental abilities
— explaining logical reasons for your expectations (first find out the characteristics, the abilities, and the expectations for a child of that age)

References for Moral Development:

Alexander, A. M., *The Money World of Your Preschooler,* East Lansing, Mich.: Cooperative Extension Science, Michigan State University, 1967.

Brophy, Jere E., Thomas L. Good, and Shari E. Nedler, *Teaching in the Preschool,* New York: Harper and Row Publishers, 1975.

Foster, C. J., *Developing Responsibility in Children,* Chicago: Science Research Associates, Inc., 1953.

Hainstock, Elizabeth G., *Teaching Montessori in the Home,* New York: Random House, 1971.

Kohlberg, L., "Development of Moral Character and Moral Ideology," in M. Hoffman and L. Hoffman, eds., *Review of Child Development Research,* vol. 1, New York: Russell Sage, 1964.

Montessori, M., *The Discovery of the Child,* translated by M. J. Costelloe, Notre Dame, Ind.: Fides Publishers, 1967.

Mussen, P. H., J. J. Conger, and J. Kagan, *Child Development and Personality,* New York: Harper and Row Publishers, 1969.

Smart, Mollie, and Russell C. Smart, *Preschool Children: Development and Relationships,* New York: Macmillan, 1973.

Sutton-Smith, B., *Child Psychology,* Englewood Cliffs, N.J.: Prentice-Hall, Inc., 1973.

Unger, S. M., "A Behavior Theory Approach to the Emergence of Guilt Reactivity in the Child," *Journal of Psychology,* 5, 1964, 85–101.

Index

Author Index

The numbers following each entry refer to pages in this volume where material is quoted or cited. The boldface type refers to the page where author is cited in bibliography.